THE
WITHERING
CHILD

THE
WITHERING
CHILD

John A. Gould

The University of Georgia Press

Athens & London

Published by the University of Georgia Press
Athens, Georgia 30602
© 1993 by John A. Gould

Designed by Kathi L. Dailey
Set in Sabon by Tseng Information Systems, Inc.
Printed and bound by Arcata Graphics
The paper in this book meets the guidelines for permanence
and durability of the Committee on Production Guidelines for
Book Longevity of the Council on Library Resources.

Printed in the United States of America

97   96   95   94   93   C   5   4   3   2   1

Library of Congress Cataloging in Publication Data
Gould, John A., 1944–
    The withering child / John A. Gould.
        p.   cm.
    Includes bibliographical references.
    ISBN 0-8203-1560-5 (alk. paper)
    1. Gould, Gardner—Health.   2. Anorexia in children—
Patients—Biography.   3. Anorexia in children—Patients—
Family relationships.   4. Gould, John A., 1944–   —Family.
I. Title.
RJ399.A6G68   1993
618.92′85′2620092—dc20
[B]   93-12351

British Library Cataloging in Publication Data available

"Abraham to kill him," by Emily Dickinson, is reprinted by
permission of the publishers and the Trustees of Amherst College
from *The Poems of Emily Dickinson,* Thomas H. Johnson, ed.,
Cambridge, Mass.: The Belknap Press of Harvard University
Press, © 1951, 1955, 1979, 1983 by the President and Fellows of
Harvard College.

For my family

O what can ail thee, Knight at arms,
  Alone and palely loitering?
The sedge is wither'd from the Lake
  And no birds sing!

—John Keats,
  "La Belle Dame Sans Merci"

ACKNOWLEDGMENTS

As I hope this book makes abundantly clear, I owe thanks to more people than I can count. I can, however, offer specific and grateful acknowledgment to those who helped me while I was writing and revising. Al Hart, Peter Koenig, David McKain, Kent Nelson, Randy Peffer, Bruce Smith, Diana Wood, and Phil Zaeder gave particular criticism; others—Vic Henningsen, Garth Hite, Pete Joel, Susan McCaslin, Don McNemar, Susan Noble, David Rodger, Jeanne Shinto, Chris and Carmel Rodriguez-Walter, to name a few—provided more general encouragement. But most important by far was the assistance of Jane, who brought me back to the truth as often as she could, as hard as it was to tell.

PROLOGUE

This story appears to be that of my five-year-old son, who during six weeks in England became anorexic while the family was on sabbatical. Upon reading and reflection, one may conclude that the narrative has not been my son's—who, after all, was too young to tell it—but more generally my family's, as we all were forced to cope with events neither we nor anyone to whom we turned for help understood. Actually it is my story, and it is true. Listen.

THE
WITHERING
CHILD

1

*T*he day we arrive in England is August 13. There are four of us, my wife Jane and I and our two sons: Gardner, the older, five and a half; and Sam, the younger, sixteen months. We have brought an ark of luggage, eight huge pieces (three holding parts of my computer—keyboard, printer, monitor) and countless handheld items: backpacks, bags of toys and books, a briefcase, diaper bag. Although we were sure the flight would be a madhouse, we seem to have survived, especially the boys. We sat in the front row of the rear cabin, where they slept at our feet just beneath the movie screen, oblivious to the images of murder and mayhem flickering above them. Still, as we lurch down the steps to the tarmac and climb onto the transport bus in Gatwick's ten o'clock sunshine (which is our five o'clock dawn back home), Gardner starts to whine. I sense a tantrum approaching, a thunderhead rolling across the horizon.

"I have leg cramps."

We are wedged among fellow passengers. If he loses control

here, there is no room to cope with him, especially as we are weighted down with all the hand luggage.

"Just sit on the floor, right by the step."

"I have leg cramps."

"Try to relax."

I look down at him sitting on the edge of the step, a forest of legs surrounding him. His hair is the color of dark honey. He has a double crown; at the top of his head, hair swirls in two little spirals as if someone set a Mixmaster against his scalp.

How would I describe him to an English neighbor, to prepare the neighbor to love and understand him as I do—especially given that at this instant he seems poised on the edge of collapse? Given the flight and the new country, what child wouldn't be having leg cramps? It is always difficult—perhaps impossible—to describe our own children fairly and objectively. Aside from lack of distance and everything else, it's hard to stay consistent about them, for they change so radically so often, as they respond to changes in landscape, in weather, in mood. We want them to be good, even when they may not be, and we look always for silver linings to their surliness.

He is a handsome, almost beautiful little boy: hazel eyes, sometimes gray, sometimes green; cleanly cut features with a great capacity for expression. Not fat, he is nonetheless sturdy, always ranking in the upper percentiles in height and weight for his age. Stubborn, strong-willed, perceptive, fiercely loyal: even from infancy he has demonstrated an altogether formidable personality. By comparison the younger boy is a tub of butter.

Beyond him, beyond all the legs, I can see through the bus's glass door the pavement rushing by. Gardner is studying the same view, for his head jerks when a baggage train flashes by in the other direction. Soon enough we are getting off the bus.

The interior of our section of Gatwick is shiny floor tile and lemon partition. The ceiling looks like that of every other airport in the world, unfinished, with strut work hanging down from the roof. Signs direct different categories of citizenship in different directions.

Somehow we get into the immigration line. My wife takes Sam somewhere to change his diapers, while his brother and I stay put. He is at peace now, sucking his thumb, sitting on the floor in a position restful for him but one that makes me wince every time I see it: knees together, legs splayed to the sides behind him, toes pointed. "How are your legs, bud?"

"Better."

I have all the critical documents in my jacket pocket: passports, British bank statement, letters between me and the dean of faculty at my school describing my sabbatical and my project. It will be independent; although I'll be near Oxford attending lectures, I won't be registered as a student. It will be a year of reading, traveling, and writing.

As I explain all this, the woman checking us in furrows her brows. "You see, I don't know what to call you."

"I'm a teacher in America."

"Yes. But you aren't a teacher here. Nor a student, apparently."

"Don't you have a category for an independent researcher?"

At last she decides she does, or has some other designation to describe me, and proceeds to stand and write and tear and file and fold. "Have a good year," she tells us. I thank her profusely, feeling somewhat jubilant at overcoming this hurdle. Just after we pass through her gate, however, I realize that I have left the brief-case on the plane. It contains our American bank statements and checks, tax information, correspondence, materials for articles I'm working on, keys and a bill of sale for a car I've bought to use here.

"Oh, shit," I explain to my wife.

3

Surely the experience of losing luggage, even critical material, is a relatively common one among all travelers. Indeed, it has happened often enough to me that I can keep most of my composure whenever I face the prospect of explaining such a loss to the disinterested employees of various public transportation operations. Earlier this summer I dropped my wallet in a men's room in South Station in Boston; realizing this fact twenty minutes later on the subway headed to Cambridge, I turned around and raced back, whimpering all the way. When I inquired, desperate, at the lost-and-found, the attendant (who was himself astonished at this event) produced it, telling me that someone had turned it in, leaving even its twenty-dollar bill untouched. Miracles happen.

Our airline is a charter affair, Trans National Travel—TNT, indeed—and three people conveying a remarkable combination of harassment and ennui sit behind a small counter, amid great mess. It is not far from the carousels delivering baggage.

I explain my predicament to a young woman.

"The telephones are all busy now, sir," she says.

As I gather together our mass of checked luggage—which fills two heavy stainless-steel airport carts—I periodically return to her. Finally she has news for me. "I'm sorry, sir. They have cleaned the plane. No briefcase was found."

My heart sinks deeper. "Perhaps someone will turn it in. Took it by mistake."

She looks at me, surprised that I have managed to dress myself. "Maybe."

"Could I have your telephone number to call to check in a day or two?"

Reluctantly she writes something on a slip of paper. We wheel the overloaded carts through customs. The trail to ground transportation leads up and down ramps, across covered parking areas, into increasing layers of darkness, until somehow we find a row of buses in the gloom beneath a long roof. Jane takes Sam into an office to ask directions; a passerby tells me that at the end of the line is a bus bound for Oxford. I tightrope the carts, each in turn, along the long thin traffic island, balancing on the very edge of the curbing, squeezing somehow past posts and queues for other buses, until finally Gardner and I reach the right one, where Jane and Sam discover us. I have thirty pounds in sterling for ground transportation, and I have no idea if it is enough. The bus driver is young, bespectacled, sweaty, and fat.

"How much does it cost to take us to Oxford?" I feel apologetic. "We've got a fair bit of luggage."

He looks us over. "How much does it cost? How much do you have?" He smiles with delight.

"Not a lot."

"The four of you? And the boy there. Tell me he'll be five tomorrow."

I don't understand. "He'll be five tomorrow?"

"Just so. That'll be twenty pounds."

I look out the window the whole way, trying to imagine myself driving in this country on the wrong side of the road, a feat I'll have to accomplish if the car keys and the bill of sale can ever be reclaimed. Every now and then I moan softly, under my breath, hopeful that my wife doesn't hear, while outside green fields roll by, splashed with sunshine and the shadows of clouds.

By Oxford the day has grown overcast and misty. We requisition two cabs to move us and our several hundred pounds of equipment eight miles north to Woodstock, where we have rented a house. We find it, and the next-door neighbor supplies us with a key, and magically we are inside. Food has been left for us—tea and coffee, cans of soup and spaghetti, frozen vegetables, even a chocolate cake—so we cook supper. We perform these seemingly impossible tasks, if not with grace, at least with efficiency; but still the absence of my briefcase hangs like an albatross around the necks of all my spirits.

We have rented a fine house, Hereford House, small but fine enough to have a name instead of a street number. It is stone, built within the past forty years, with a steep slate roof. On the ground floor to the left of the entrance is a kitchen, to the right a living room, and straight ahead a so-called "warm" room, containing a washer, dryer, clothesline, and water heater. On what I must learn to call the first floor are a master bedroom, two smaller ones for the boys, and a bathroom. On the second floor is another bedroom, a second bath, and storage.

Hereford House belongs to a colleague of mine and his wife, Chris and Carmel Walter, friends with two children, who have left the house completely furnished. Their son is a contemporary of Gardner; their daughter two years older. "This is William's room," Jane tells him. "Do you want to sleep here, or in Sophia's?"

He considers carefully, a Harvard MBA graduate choosing an office at the new firm. "I would like Sophia's, I think. It's bigger."

"Fine," says Jane. "Now you can start unpacking your toys."

Outside is the "garden"—*yard* in American—which is triangular, surrounded by a seven-foot cedar fence, blocking all view of the street. It is a huge playpen, really, equipped with a Quadro climbing structure and plastic balls, bats, and other toys. Next door is a small convenience store, just beyond that the Woodstock Primary School where in a month Gardner will begin his first year of formal education.

In the apex of the garden's triangle, farthest from the house, is a white wrought-iron table with four white wrought-iron chairs set about in the grass. Small sparse trees, shrubs, flowers, and herbs are planted along the base of the fence; grist for the mill of the younger boy, I think at once. Jane looks at the table and chairs with satisfaction. "Ah," she says smiling. "Afternoon tea."

It continues cloudy and warm as we unpack. The boys are excited, and we send them out into the garden to play. After a time Gardner calls me out. "Look, Dad."

He climbs onto the Quadro, which is a sort of plastic jungle gym made of red tubes. Colored plastic squares can be snapped into the interstices of the grid. Thus it can form a little play-house, or a series of levels, or whatever. Its present shape is a whatever, long and irregular like a tiny skyscraper turned on its side. He swings himself up, hooks his legs over a bar, and hangs upside down.

"Terrific," I say. "Just like a monkey."

"Gog," says Sam in excitement.

I follow his attention. The back of the store next door has outside stairs leading up to the living quarters above; a black boarder collie and a fat blond lab are looking across the fence at us from their landing.

"Right, Sam! Good work! Goggies!"

"Goggie," he agrees with me.

Our first two pieces of official business are to register with the Thames Valley Police and to obtain library cards. Both institutions are right up the road from Hereford House. We go first to the police station, which is behind the library.

"Why do we need to go to the police, Dad?" asks Gardner.

"We need to get something called 'Alien Registration Cards.' "

"Aliens? Like E.T.? Are we aliens?"

"Sort of," says Jane. "That means our real home is in America."

We speak to Police Constable Lee, a friendly young officer, who explains that we must return sometime in a fortnight or so with passport-sized photographs and sixty pounds. Then we go around front to the library, which is a large single-floor room of shelves and a couple of small offices tucked behind the counter. There we are asked for some bit of proof—a bill, perhaps—that we live in Woodstock. As luck would have it, I am carrying the morning's second mail, a bill from Southern Electric, Cotswold Divisional Office, stating that I must pay a deposit of seventy-five pounds or the electricity will be shut off. Such institutional bullying commands the respect of the librarians, who quickly and seriously fill out our applications.

The library is a small branch, not many thousands of books, but a new and cheerful building with a photocopying machine and a microfiche catalog linking it with other Oxfordshire libraries. On the shelves I find Park Honan's biography of Jane Austen and a copy of *Emma,* both of which I check out. The Hereford House library contains *Persuasion,* which I am mostly through. Most of my own books are, of course, back home.

Some contemporary of Dickens may have devised the Woodstock Library's check-out system. Each borrower is given five gray cardboard sleeves, triangular in shape, endorsed with name and address. When I present my books, I hand the librarian also two sleeves; she takes out the cards from the back of the books, stamps the due date on them and in the books too, and slips a sleeve over each card, filing it in a long thin wooden box. Thus no borrower can take more than five books, because no borrower is given more than five sleeves.

Gardner receives five blue sleeves and takes home three books for himself, two about knights and one about sailing and monsters, and two other books for Sam, chunky cardboard ones with pictures of animals. "Sometime soon we should visit a castle, don't you think?" I ask him as we walk back.

"What?" he replies.

"A castle. Where the knights lived. They have them here in England. Real ones."

"Sure," he says. "I guess so."

            The most impressive attraction of the town of Woodstock is not a castle, but a palace, Blenheim, the seat of the Duke of Marlborough. Built over the seventeen years between 1705 and 1722 under the vision and supervision of the talented Sir John Vanbrugh, an eighteenth-century architect-playwright, it was a royal gift to the first Duke for having defeated Tallard at Blenheim in 1704. The park covers 2,100 acres. Winston Churchill, a cousin of the ninth Duke, was born there in 1874. And now, more than a century later, as residents of the town, we are entitled to stroll there too and range the grounds almost as freely as young Winnie did.

A day or two after our arrival, having asked at the library about how to go about it, we set out to apply for a "Walking Permit." The park entrance is about a half mile from Hereford House, up through the town. So off we go, up past the library and the police and fire stations, across the A34, down High Street past the Coop (the largest market in town) and the Bear Hotel and our bank, Sam in the stroller, Gardner behind us grousing about the walk.

"My legs have cramps."

"You know, dear," Jane says, "you just aren't used to walking. In America we seem to drive everywhere we go."

"How come we don't drive here?" He is using the voice I call Le Misérable, a self-pitying grumble that can modulate in an instant into an even more hopeless tone, the Desperate Whiner.

"Because we don't have a car yet."

"How come?"

But when we come to the huge stone gate for the first time, even Le Misérable turns silent. "Head straightaway to the palace," says the guard. "To the left of the main entrance is the estate manager's office. They'll issue you a permit. You'll need something with your name and address on it."

We nod, prepared for this, and pass through. The road sweeps across the front of the palace, two or three hundred yards away; to our right the grass falls to a lake that narrows where a handsome stone bridge crosses it. Ducks, geese, and swans dot the water. Cows and sheep are grazing all around us, organic clippers keeping the lawns trimmed close. The palace spreads out wider and wider as we approach, its rectangular masses of sandy-colored stone spiked to the ground with low square towers. The grass is brown from the summer's drought, as yet unrelieved with the year moving into autumn. I look down at Sam. His mouth is open in astonishment and he points toward the animals.

"Sheep," I tell him.

"Yay," says his brother enthusiastically. "Sheep. Cows. Sheep."

"Eep."

"Hey, Mom, he said it."

"That's right, *sheep*."

2

My wife is a priest in the Episcopal Church. This status makes her unusual in the United States, virtually unheard of in Great Britain, where she is an as-yet unevolved species, a mammal in the Age of Dinosaurs. In 1974 in Philadelphia, when Jane was eighteen years old, eleven women deacons knelt before three brave retired bishops, who laid their hands on the women's heads, thereby transforming them into priests. The bishops were all retired; none of the active ones would break the block, so to speak. Although they did not have the permission of the diocesan episcopate to ordain these women, they still had the power, and their quiet revolution is called today the "irregular ordination" of the Philadelphia Eleven. The next year a number of women priests were regularly ordained, and the old boy network in the House of Bishops began to yield to the inevitable. My wife began seminary when we were married in 1982 and was ordained as a deacon in 1986 and as a priest a year later. Two of her professors in seminary, Sue Hiatt and Carter Heyward, were members of the Philadelphia Eleven.

Her name, Jane, is the feminine version of my own, which means "God is gracious." In my first dictionary, a 1956 *Webster's Collegiate,* there was an appendix of "Common English Given Names," in which I first learned that people's names usually denote something beyond their owners' singularity. "God is gracious": I remember being quite pleased that my name meant this. I still have the dictionary; a few years ago, thumbing through it, I noticed that the definition of *space ship* is "an imaginary vehicle of the future."

"God is gracious" notwithstanding, in earlier years I would never have imagined myself married to a member of the clergy. We met at a school where we were both teaching, and we started going to Red Sox games together. When I began to express myself in more serious terms, she took me aside. "There's one thing you should know right away about me. I'm quite sure that in the next few years I want to leave teaching and go to seminary. I want to be an Episcopal priest."

I was stunned, but only for a moment. At once I saw I'd have to return to churchgoing, a habit I'd fallen away from since highschool, some two decades earlier. Please understand: I don't believe myself a hypocrite. I loved her. I have never been a rebel; nothing in the teachings of the church I grew up in ever repelled me. It has usually honored behavior I believe good, while both it and I mostly agree on the actions I ought to be ashamed of. During the sixties and seventies, however, Sunday mornings simply found me elsewhere: in bed, or somewhere outdoors, or driving long distances back from a weekend to wherever I was employed at the time. Now I had to return to morning worship—so I hoped with a certain amount of gracefulness, if not grace itself. Having always enjoyed bathtub singing and lately having felt some desire to learn to read music, in a flash of inspiration I joined the choir at St. Michael's, the local Episcopal church.

And then we married. I came to teach English at a large, old, wonderfully well endowed school, and my wife went to seminary in Cambridge. Toward the second year of our marriage—after very little effort on our part—she discovered that she was pregnant.

My musical avocation continued apace, and although I had left the choir at St. Michael's, I was singing regularly in three arenas: a barbershop quartet, the school's chorus, and a mixed quartet I had initiated in the English department. This last began when I showed three colleagues—a soprano, an alto, and a bass, as it turned out—four of Emily Dickinson's poems that I had set to hymns. Such liberty is by no means an original idea—I can recall a professor in college telling us that Dickinson used common meter ironically, to bite against the sanctity of church tunes—but original or not, the effect of hearing "Abraham to kill him" set against "Onward, Christian Soldiers" is both amusing and wicked.

So, calling ourselves "The Dickinsingers," the four of us began to sing. We learned a number of other settings for poems, and in the spring, as the tenth graders were all embarking on the study of poetry, we gave an afternoon concert. The auditorium was packed, probably because many teachers had required their classes to come hear us. We were none of us at all "professional" singers. Still, we handled our music—by such composers as Samuel Barber, Thomas Morley, and Vincent Persichetti, in addition to the hymnists—well enough to feel a surge of elation after we finished. I remember our soprano, a handsome young woman with a rich *mezzo* quality to her voice, soaring confidently up to her D of "Oh, Star," in Randall Thompson's setting of Frost's "Choose Something Like a Star." The students seemed enthusiastic. Afterward we trooped down to the Inn, where in a confluence of emotions I ordered a bottle of champagne.

When the bottle came, I said, "Guess what. Jane's pregnant."

"Cheers," said everyone, and the soprano added, "You'll have to name the baby Emily."

From that moment of rejoicing in late afternoon sunshine on the terrace of the Inn, drinking champagne with the Dickinsingers, our first child was going to be a girl and her name was going to be Emily. I don't recall having any previous desire for a girl—indeed most of my adult life had seemed to be focused on avoiding children rather than creating them—but furiously I manufactured for myself images of Emily: in blue shorts darting about a soccer field, in a white tutu dancing *Swan Lake*, in a sweater and rumpled skirt winning the Yale Younger Poets Award.

The next September I became a dean at the school, and Jane entered her third year of seminary. Her body ballooned with Emily, who kicked and entrechatted and wrote prenatal couplets beneath my terrified hand during the nights. Finally, four days into the New Year, at 5:00 A.M., I drove Jane into Boston and sat with her in a labor room all morning. When the birth came early in the afternoon, I nearly fainted, for I was utterly unprepared for a son.

The next day I wrote a sort of sonnet:

> A circus clown, launched from the cannon of
> Your mother's womb, you soared across the gulf
> That separates will be from is, and dropped
> Lightly in the doctor's outstretched arms.
> You, called Emily all your unborn life,
> Mooned us with your scrotal sac and rump,
> Bewailed in tears and other bitter terms
> Indignities too vague and dark for words.
> Once born in grace and grease, my angry clown,
> You simmered down—to nurses' swabs and swaddles,

Your mother's trembling breast, even my knees—
As sweet sleep sang you back to what you'd left.
None of us has words for pain or joy.
("It's a boy," was all I sobbed. "A boy.")

I had not the foggiest idea what we should call him. His
entire presence had undone me; the French have a word, *boule-
verser,* which describes me perfectly, bowl-versed, knocked like
ninepins, knees atremble. Somehow we decided to name him
after my father, who was named after his father, the names themselves coming not from a dictionary appendix, but from various
surnames which had at some time or other entered our family:
Gardner Sabin.

For four years afterward he had us to himself, a handsome,
intelligent, exceedingly intense child. Even as we loved him, we
recognized his strength of will. His day-care teachers reported
that he could not be redirected; when he wanted a toy, he would
persist—sometimes quietly, sometimes not—for an hour until he
got it. He slept very soundly. If awakened prematurely, he would
sometimes kick and cry inconsolably. Once in a while, the screams
nearly shattered glass.

His earliest loves were trucks and other large machines.
"Uck!" he would cry from his stroller, and heads would jerk
around; sure enough, a flatbed or a moving van would be rolling by. One day in the fall when he was not yet three, I arrived
at the day-care center to pick him up. By the door was a large
sheet of red poster board on which was written, "THIS THANKS-
GIVING I AM THANKFUL"—and underneath were all the children's names, with their responses. Answers were mostly similar:
"For My Grandmother and Grandfather," "For My Family," "For
My Dog Sparky," and so on. Beside "Gardner" was testimony to
his unswerving fidelity: "For Backhoes and Dumptrucks."

When Jane discovered herself pregnant a second time, we were concerned about him. "I think he may have trouble with a new Emily," she said.

"Not Emily," I said. "I don't want to know its name until it arrives. I'm not going through that again."

We worked to prepare him, talking up enthusiastically a new brother or sister, reading him books about children—some of them about badger or bear children, to be sure—getting him used to such arrivals. We took him to a class for new siblings at the hospital, where he walked around, saw some new babies, and got to play with a life-sized baby doll. Afterward, one of the teachers spoke to us. "I thought you might want to know. He beat up the doll."

The second boy was born on Easter Sunday, after my wife had celebrated the nine and eleven o'clock Eucharists. We named him Samuel, which means "his name is El," *El* being a Hebrew word meaning *God*. I have always loved the Biblical story of Samuel, the little boy in Eli's temple who, awakened by God's voice, runs to Eli asking, "What is it, master?"

Much to our relief the older boy initially reacted to the younger with excitement, even joy. I carry a picture in my wallet of the two of them, a day-old infant in a white blanket clutching his brother's tee shirt, while the brother holds him on his knees, laughing with glee at the red bumpy face beneath his own.

The younger boy has proved more relaxed than the older— more of a humorist, a Will Rogers to his brother's Mort Sahl, or to put the matter into literary terms, an E. B. White to his Dorothy Parker. He also has proved to be a barfer, which his brother never was; especially after a feeding of milk, more especially if he had a cold, there would come up a belch and a handful of slimy white. One morning last Christmas vacation, when he was about nine months old, Sam and I were home alone together while the others worked or schooled. He was crawling about the living room, inspecting the tree. I snuck into the downstairs toilet, leaving the door open, desperately hoping no one would come calling. All at once he realized I was no longer with him.

"Unghh!" he called out.

"I'm here," I shouted, and he stuck his head around the corner at the other end of the hall.

"Unghh!" he said again.

"Come here, buddy." He crawled to me quickly, fluidly, like a fish swims. Leaning over, I picked him up and patted him. "There, there."

"*Blep*." As I bent forward to see what now lay glistening in my underwear, he snuggled into the crook of my neck, not in triumph, but merely in joy.

Since Jane's ordination, to my untrained and perhaps subjective eye she has done wonderfully well. For the last four years she was an assistant in a parish north of Boston, and they loved her there. She was in charge of the Church School program, which burgeoned under her direction with thirty-some teachers, an integrated curriculum, and more than a hundred children. She preached to both the children and the adults with intelligence. When the rector retired last Thanksgiving, she took charge of the congregation until the interim pastor arrived in January. Somehow she got the parish through the retirement, the Advent season, and the horrific death of the music director from AIDS—one of the darkest preparations for the Messiah's birthday I've ever been witness to.

Successful and happy as she was there, she hadn't been preparing for England without a certain amount of relief. Whenever a rector leaves a church, it's almost inevitable that the other clergy do, too. Even if this were not the custom, Jane would have left anyway; her career at this parish had clearly reached its climax, and she was drained. When the sabbatical became certain, she turned to England with me, for Episcopal traditions are Anglican, and she knew there was much she could accomplish in England, in Oxford, even in Woodstock.

We waste no time in going into Oxford. The bus costs two pounds return, which means round-trip. Gardner is half-fare, Sam rides free. So we travel high along the A34, the flat green fields stretching out broadly on either side. I notice a bike path beside the road. Between Woodstock and Oxford are a couple of little villages—Yarnton, its name suggesting to me the wool industry, and Begbroke, perhaps reminiscent of some sadder tale of poverty and mendicancy.

We roll into the same bus depot where three days earlier we arrived with all our baggage. Now we swing down with just a stroller. "Anyone have to go to the bathroom?" Jane asks, ever mindful of the needs of others. Gardner says, "Yes." I have already become aware of England's great thoughtfulness in placing public toilet facilities abundantly and, by American standards, cleanly.

We then wander about looking for some way to get passport-sized pictures for our alien registration. Cornmarket Street, one of the two main streets in the city center, seems to be open only to buses, bicycles, and pedestrians. There are department stores, shoe stores, clothing stores, record stores. There is a Burger King. There is a McDonald's. In one of the department stores we find a photo machine. The boys love its drapery and flashing lights, but they are hungry too, so while we wait for our images to develop,

Jane goes off to forage, returning with some sandwiches and soft drinks. We eat outside on a bench in front of what turns out to be the college called Christ Church.

Later we stroll back up Cornmarket toward the Martyrs' Monument, a spire set on the street to honor Bishops Ridley and Lattimore and Archbishop Cranmer, who were burnt for heresy by agents of Queen Mary Tudor in the sixteenth century. Statues of the three men stand in niches. From a distance the monument might seem to be a church in the process of growing out of the ground. I stand below it, looking up into one of the bishops' mournful faces. The stone was once beige-colored, but the soot and exhaust of centuries in Oxford has blackened it, as if the martyrs have been removed from their fires seared and scorched.

Much more to the excitement of the boys, we decide to take the Oxford Tour, a fleet of double-decker buses with open tops ubiquitous throughout the city. The day has turned glowery and gray, so the bus is nearly empty when we enter, and up top we sit in front, just under the gaze of the young man with the microphone. "On your right is the Ashmolean Museum, founded by Elias Ashmole in 1677," he is saying. "It contains one of the finest collections of curios in the world. I urge you to visit it before you leave Oxford."

As the tour proceeds, he urges us to visit other Oxford institutions as well: Blackwell's bookstore, the Bodlean Library, Christ Church, especially when the choir is singing. This last setting, close to where we joined the tour, is where we ate lunch; and, taking his advice, we climb down to walk through the college gardens open to the public. Sam falls asleep in the stroller as the skies come clear and sunlight slants across the grass and the stone walls.

"Maybe I can come in here some afternoon for evensong," says Jane. I nod encouragingly, smiling at her and the two boys; we are here for a year; we have all the time in the world; there will be nothing we cannot do beneath and among these dreaming spires.

3

---

*D*awn Templeton: the name
dances before my joyful eyes, a lovely name with connotations
of breaking day and rosy light, villages of houses of worship,
churches and mosques and synagogues. Three days after we arrived, I called back to my school for the telephone location of the
colleague I bought our car from, the keys to which were lost with
the briefcase. I knew he had left another set in Cambridge with
one of his former neighbors, who is looking after the car until I
show up.

"Dawn Templeton," said the Dean of Faculty's secretary.

"What's that?"

"Dawn Templeton. She's a stewardess for the airline you flew
over on."

"No kidding."

"She called us. I spoke to her. She found your briefcase."

Weight I hadn't measured melted from my shoulders. I
thought of the notes for an article on Venezuelan orchids I was

---

writing, of the checks and receipts and savings bonds, of car keys and papers, and I said, "Thank Christ."

"How are you guys doing?"

"Better since talking to you. What's she going to do with it?"

The secretary didn't know. "Maybe she'll put it on a plane and send it over. She didn't give me a number or an address, but I gave her yours."

As soon as I hung up, I picked up Sam and did a turn through the living room. "Dawn Templeton!" I sang. "Oh, Dawn, Dawn Templeton!"

Gardner looked up from an afternoon television program. "Who?"

"Dawn Templeton. She found the briefcase!"

"Who is she?"

"She is a stewardess. Hey, Gardie. We're gonna get our car!"

"Good." He turned back to the set.

I put Sam down and called the airline. The voice at the other end of the wire sounded as if it had just rolled out of bed. I began to identify myself.

"I lost a briefcase on the Boston–Gatwick flight last week."

"Right."

"I've just heard that one of your stewardesses found it."

"Is that so?"

"Yes. A Dawn Templeton. Bless her. She called my employer back in the States."

"Dawn Templeton, you say?"

"Yes. Does she work for you?"

"I don't know, sir." He paused. "She might. What's her address?"

"I don't know. She didn't say, apparently. Can't you find out and help her get the bag back to me?"

"Look, sir. Why don't I try to find out for you and ring you back?"

"Yes, wonderful."

Almost the identical conversation ensued the next day, with a different, though equally laconic, voice. This time the respondent did call back. "Look, sir, it seems this Templeton woman does work for us. She's based in America. I've sent over a request, and she should be getting in touch with you soon."

"Wait. Can't you get her to ship it back to you folks and let me come to Gatwick and pick it up?"

"I don't know about that, sir. I'll ask that she send it to you somehow. Just be patient."

I am a patient person by nature. One of my hobbies is photographing wildflowers—as I recently did on that trip to Venezuela—and I have sat for an hour waiting for a patch of light to move across a forest floor to illuminate a blossom. One summer I rode a bicycle from Maine to Seattle, Washington, alone, taking three months to complete the trek. I have spent six years writing a novel, although it is true I taught school and otherwise kept alive during this period. Somewhere, somehow, during my life I have learned how to wait.

There are two postal deliveries each day in Woodstock, even on Saturday. Each day I wait for the sound of letters dropping through the slot, hoping that the doorbell will ring with a package. Part of me knows it won't, for surface mail will take a month, and airmail will cost the earth, and Dawn Templeton doesn't know us from Adam and Eve, doesn't know how grateful we will be to receive that briefcase. Today is Saturday, and there is nothing in the mail, no briefcase, no letters, no bills, nothing.

24

It is about eleven-thirty, and Jane has gone downtown, not yet returned. As I stand at the gate, musing about the post, a woman's voice beside me says, "Excuse me. Are you one of the new residents of Hereford House?"

"Yes."

"I'm Jane Brown. We live across the street." She cannot be within two inches of five feet tall, yet she is not tiny, not frail, indeed not without presence, wearing a red turtleneck and old tan corduroy trousers. Round face, blonde pageboy hair, clear blue eyes, freckles on her nose, she smiles at me as if she has been waiting patiently for me to return to her, as if I am an old friend perhaps or a lover from a distant past, whom she still remembers with amusement and affection. I am at once taken, won utterly.

"I've been meaning to stop over to see how you were making out. We heard all about you from the Walters. How are you finding the old place? I meant to stop over sooner, but I've been away and we're as usual in something of a muddle."

"It's been very nice."

"It's frightfully late notice, I know, but we'd love to have you over for Sunday dinner, actually. My mother is coming from Bristol. I'm doing a pork roast. Do you folks eat meat?"

"What?" Things seem to be happening very quickly. With relief I see my wife coming down the street. "Look," I say. "Here comes my Jane."

On Sunday we rise bright and early on our first Sabbath morning to discover the workings of the Lord in the land of Lattimore and Cranmer and Ridley. "There's a children's service at nine, I saw yesterday," Jane tells us all.

"I don't want to go," says Gardner.

"We should all go to church together," she says. "I never get a

---

chance to sit with you guys. It'll be fun."

"It's not fair."

"Come on," I say. "It's a nice day."

We walk through the warm morning air. The church is a block short of the Blenheim Palace gate, so Sam sits in the stroller happily, anticipating eep and goggies, while his brother walks grumpily but wordlessly along. At last we turn in at the gate of St. Mary Magdalene, Woodstock: fourteenth century, a square bell-tower, the numerals on the clock freshly gilded, the brown stones going black, deeply scarred by acid rain. The grill to the vestibule is ajar, the door unlocked; but the nave is empty and silent.

"Oh, shoot," says Jane, looking at a sheet pinned by the door.

"What is it, Mommy?"

"The children's service is in Bladon. I never noticed. I didn't know they had services there."

"Where?"

"Bladon, sweetie. It's a town on the other side of the palace."

"Let's go inside," I say.

Despite the requisite air of serenity and one or two lovely stained glass windows, St. Mary Magdalene's does not look particularly fancy. What do catch my eyes, however, are the kneeling cushions beneath every pew, their embroidered covers bright as newly minted pennies. I pick one up with a lamb on it, dated 1984. "Look," I say to Sam.

"Eep!"

"These must have kept the women of the parish busy," says Jane, looking at some others. "They all seem to have been done over a three-year stretch."

"An active altar guild."

Down in the front pew I discover cushions for the Duke of Marlborough, the Duchess, and—complete with an embroidered portrait—Winston Churchill. "How often do you suppose Winnie attends services nowadays?" I ask Jane.

In the rear the boys discover a small table with two or three chairs of a similar scale and a box of old toys. Gardner begins fitting together the pieces of a worn puzzle.

"This is probably the church school," she says, resignation in her voice. "This doesn't look like a parish with lots for the children." My mind slips back to the church we left, a warren of ten or so classrooms beneath the parish hall, teeming with parents and children in the few minutes before the start of the adult service.

We walk out from the grace of God into the warm sun. "Yay," says Gardner. "No church today."

I am standing next to the gate to Hereford House looking over the wall into the street. Jane has gone back to the church by herself, not trusting that those children's facilities will keep our boys ruly enough so they won't turn the service into suet. Gardner is watching television inside although the day is fair; behind me Sam is diddling with a mostly inflated rubber ball with green-and-white pentagons printed on it, an infant soccer ball. I go back into the house.

"Hey. Let's go kick Sam's soccer ball over at the field." There is a town soccer field—say "football pitch," here—just around the corner behind us.

"O.K., Dad. Maybe I'll see my friend."

My heart sinks. A group of three boys have been rocketing around the neighborhood on bicycles. He has decided that one of them is his friend. They are older, maybe eight or nine, and a couple of nights ago we were over beside the football pitch with a whiffle ball and bat when they turned up. They were fascinated with the idea of baseball, and we showed them how to hit. All three of them wanted to keep the bat at their feet and golf up, as if they were playing cricket. Everyone played enthusiastically, but I don't think they were as excited about us as Gardner was about them. I haven't seen any of them since.

The field is deserted and we kick the ball around for a few minutes. It's a mown hay field, really, the grass growing sparsely, especially around the goals. Sam loves balls and hoots after this one, but Gardner scuffs at it once or twice and then turns away.

"I'm tired of this, Dad."

On the way back he stops to inspect some bushes. "Hey, Dad. Look." He reaches up to pick something, which he pops into his mouth. "Blackberries."

"Excellent. If we can pick enough, I'll make a pie."

We stand there, leaning over a small ditch, picking among the berries, most of which are yet green. These bramble bushes form a hedge enclosing someone's garden, personal fruit within, public without. I am feeding myself and Sam—who is grabbing at my pant leg demanding more—while Gardner is ahead of us, closer to the road that runs beside our house. Suddenly I hear him speak: "Hi!"

A small bicycle flashes by: one of the boys, in fact, the "friend." He seems to pedal all the faster when he hears Gardner's call. I feel my chest knot tight. My son's face turns impassive, like a post, and he says nothing more. I have no idea what I should do.

Gardner has never made friends easily. In his preschool he was surrounded mostly by older, thus better-behaved girls. For two years he and two other little boys were the black sheep of the outfit, measuring the success of their days by how few time-outs they were awarded. The three of them fought against each other and the system every day, pushing and shoving and punching. He still thinks of this pair as his best friends. Yet one left the preschool after the first year and has scarcely been seen since. Perhaps it wasn't a free-market friendship they shared, but a camaraderie of cellmates.

At home we have a videotape of his fifth birthday party. Hilarity runs high through it; we had six kids act out Hansel and Gretel, a story Gardner loves, especially when the witch recoils in horror at the impossibly thin chicken-bone finger Hansel sticks out at her. On the tape Gardner at first doesn't want anything to do with the production, but before long he is assuming roles from everyone, taking over as the wimpy father, finally shouldering his way into the plum role, Hansel. That is, of course, the part we wanted the birthday boy to play, but every time I watch this tape and see him knocking the others around, I think to myself, hey, be nicer. These are your friends.

It is hard to imagine two more opposite people than Jane and Martyn Brown, I am thinking as I sit at this crowded table: female to male, short to tall, fair to dark, extroverted to reserved, endo- to ectomorphic. And yet as we crunch together, their two children and ours, Jane Brown's mother, and the four of us, the warm sweet smell of roast pork soothes us, smoothing our surfaces, so that we feel no rubs, no frictions. Gardner is almost exactly of an age with Peter Brown, a flaxen-haired impish tease; Harriet, a couple years older than they, with an air of great sophistication, is clearly taken with Sam. Conversation is energetic, disconnected.

"Well, the vicar is rather an odd bird, wouldn't you say?"
"Dad, shall I let Sam have a glass of juice?"

"Which Turtle do you like?"

"I really haven't heard him. I liked the woman today, though."

"Perhaps you should ask John."

"Donatello."

"Sure, Harriet. But don't fill it too full. He isn't very reliable."

"I like Metalhead."

"Yes, that was quite a coup, wasn't it? Mart, did you know that there was a woman leading Morning Prayer at the old church today?"

The issue of women's ordination swirls up around us all. At present the Church of England admits women to the order of deacons, and there are over a thousand women so ordained. A deacon is empowered to read the Gospel during the Eucharist and assist a priest in the celebration, but may not celebrate the Eucharist alone or absolve people's sins or pronounce a formal blessing. For the right of women to perform these offices great furor roiled the American Episcopal Church nearly two decades ago, sending some congregations spinning in the direction of schism. Today similar spasms threaten the Anglican Church in England.

At St. Mary Magdalene's this morning a woman lay reader preached, no big deal from our point of view, but a strange event for Woodstock. My wife has heard that the vicar, a staunch opponent of women's ordination at all levels, would not be likely to countenance a woman deacon in the pulpit. I can see that Jane Brown is interested, even excited, though she seems more like a Congregationalist or maybe a Unitarian—if the Colonial sects mean anything over here.

"Did you talk to her after the service?"

My mind eases back from the discussion, and I consider my surroundings. Their house, like Hereford House, seems to my American view small. The Browns live on the ground floor, in two bedrooms, a bath, a study, a living room, a kitchen with the table we are squeezed around at one end, and an odds-and-ends room by the side door. Upstairs is a small apartment, presently vacant, which contains from time to time a lodger. The house is under renovation and has the appearance of having been this way ever since the Browns moved in two years ago and of likely remaining so for quite a time longer. Lamps and tables and rummage stand in stacks in the hall. The study's wallpaper has been partly peeled off, scraps lying on dropcloths.

The kitchen looks out into the back garden through large wood-framed glass doors. It stretches a good distance: a terrace, an apple tree with a wood bench beneath, the lawn with smaller trees and shrubs placed about, a greenhouse which seems to be filled with furniture and tools, and finally a hedge way at the back.

"We have hedgehogs that come into the garden," Peter says.

"Really? Can we see them?"

"They only come out at night. One night we stayed up and saw them."

After dinner we take up our tea and coffee and move outside. The boys scamper around after a soccer ball as the adults move outdoor furniture under the apple tree, which has been dropping ugly bruised fruit onto the grass.

"Look at these, Mart," says Jane Brown. "We'll get cracking with them. They're cookers," she explains, reading my mind. "They look dreadful, but we make tarts and applesauce with them. You must feel free to take as many as you want. We can't possibly use them all."

"The boys and I found some blackberries by the road. Do you make blackberry pies?"

"Certainly do. They grow very thick up on the old railway embankment just across from your house."

"Good news," says my wife. "John bakes wonderful pies. He wrote two cookbooks."

"Really?"

"I'm afraid so," I say. "But don't be too excited. It was a long time ago, and one of them was a hundred different recipes for cooking hot dogs."

Back home in the evening, the boys in bed, Jane writing in her journal, I have just finished *Persuasion,* where Anne Elliott, the heroine, "prized the frank, the open-hearted, the eager character beyond all others." Had she known the Browns, she would have put them at once into her good graces.

But what of Dawn Templeton and the briefcase? Her name is almost an Austen one—the first a bit exotic maybe, but monosyllabic enough to fit in with Jane or Anne; the second, were she designated "Miss Templeton," a perfect choice for a strange woman arrived in the village, perhaps, or a governess with a mysterious background, although I fear I may be mixing her up with someone from Thomas Hardy.

One reading of *Persuasion*—and, indeed, of *Mansfield Park,* which I finished the other day—is that of the stranger in a strange land. Fanny Price and, to a somewhat lesser degree, Anne Elliott are trying to establish intimate human relationships with outsiders when those of family and near society have failed. Neither woman's family offers any moral support—one is poor, the other snobbish, both brainless. Fanny has to contend with the oily Henry Crawford, Anne with her even slyer cousin William Elliott. Both women use caution, necessarily, for the stakes are high—virtually life and death—as Anne's friend Mrs. Smith, nearly ruined by Elliott's machinations, shows us. Earlier Anne commented about her cousin Elliott, "They had been acquainted a month, she could not be satisfied that she really knew his character." When

---

32

you are new in a world, how do you recognize your friends, your foes, or those indifferent to you? The Browns are surely friends; Gardner's "friend" on the bicycle perhaps a foe, or at best one of the indifferent ones; and where does Dawn Templeton—who today exists only as a name—belong?

So I muse, sitting here on the couch in Hereford House, fitting Jane Brown and Dawn Templeton into the novel that our lives have been dictating, when my head suddenly spins away with the rhythm and music of Simon and Garfunkle: "Where have you gone, Miss Dawn Templeton, our family turns its lonely eyes to you, Yoo, hoo, hoo."

4

-----

*I*nspector Gadget stretches a metal tentacle from beneath his trenchcoat at one end of the living room, while at the other I take notes on Park Honan's *Jane Austen: Her Life*. The television set and the video machine play a significant role in our lives here, as well as back home. Gardner often used to watch cartoons in America; in England Dennis the Menace and He-Man and a few others have their appointed slots on the four channels, usually ITV, one of the independents.

There aren't many, thank God, for it's so hard to turn him away from the set, since his social life has been otherwise so slow. Peter Brown has been over to play once in a while, and some afternoons we go swimming in the public pool next to the secondary school down the street, but we are waiting for his school to start, hoping that there he will find a close friend. His favorite cartoon characters do not appear on British television. These are the Teenage Mutant Ninja Turtles, whose name in this country has been softened to the Teenage Mutant *Hero* Turtles. I have no idea what the word "ninja" signifies to British ears, but it must

-----

be nasty. Back home he has two Turtle videotapes, *Sky Turtles* and *Kowabunga, Shredhead.* Just before we left, I had to buy him a Turtle cup at Burger King, even though he knew we couldn't bring it here. And his figures of Leonardo, one of the Turtles, and of Rocksteady, one of the bad guys, have given him enormous status with Peter Brown.

He folds into himself when he watches, holding the satin ear of his bunny and sucking his thumb, sprawled bonelessly over the contours of the couch. If his muscles are relaxed, he can twist his legs like a contortionist, bending them back far enough to touch his toes to his ears. Every now and then a laugh flies past the plug of his thumb, but mostly he absorbs the cartoon mayhem as passively as a sponge. I wonder what gets lodged in his brain.

Afternoons I've been watching the India Test Match. Back home I love the Red Sox and going to Fenway Park; here it's cricket, which seems to me the way baseball would look if Jonas Salk had designed it instead of Abner Doubleday: white, symmetrical, elegant, with games as long and repetitive as scientific research. I am not bored a bit; it's clear the ball is often bowled with terrific speed, and when several of the fielders—only one of whom is wearing any gloves—gather close to the batsman trying to pressure him into a mistake, I fear for their fingers, their teeth, their cheekbones. Americans make fun of cricket, saying they can't understand the game, but in fact it is much clearer than the balk rule, the designated hitter, and the free agency system.

England has been having difficulty with the Indians, even though the British team this year is supposed to be a good one. Everyone is watching a player called Graham Gooch, a bearded batsman who is knocking on the doors of a number of scoring records, a good player having a great season. I watch for the details, Gooch's keeping his front elbow high so the bat stays perpendicular, for instance; this prevents hitting the ball in the air, where it can be caught. A batsman is up only once during his team's innings. Unlike baseball, an out is terminal.

At night, the children in bed, Jane and I have found a few programs that interest us. Occasionally there is a film we want to see, even to tape. Channel 3 is rebroadcasting some of the Inspector Morse series, which we saw in America. Morse is an officer of the Thames Valley Police—the same force that employs our own P. C. Lee behind the library. Morse is stationed right in Oxford, so we can see him entering the Ashmolean Museum and shortly thereafter enter it ourselves.

But the programming that most consumes us is the news, filled with military activity in the Persian Gulf, Saddam Hussein, Kuwait, Iraq, hostages, the possibility of war. It is clear we could not be in a more pro-American country at this minute, not even perhaps the United States itself. Britain, the island nation where petrol is selling for nearly two and a half pounds a gallon, is petrified at the vision of an Arab jingoist like Saddam mucking up the OPEC world. President Bush is a hero, as when the other day he called up a mess of reservists, and even the folks we meet around Woodstock seem to be nodding approvingly at us in our Captain America superhero costumes, whether we want the role or not.

From Park Honan I am learning that even demure, reserved Jane Austen was not unaware of war in her lifetime. Two of her brothers, Frank and Charles, were career naval officers who rose to the rank of admiral; thus, when in *Mansfield Park* William Price accepts the patronage of the questionable Henry Crawford and his equally questionable uncle Admiral Crawford, she demonstrates an insider's view of how one got ahead in the British navy. (Apparently patronage assisted Frank Austen's career.) I wonder now how many Lieutenant William Prices are saying good-bye to their mothers and girlfriends and sister Fannys, preparing to sail away from England into the gathering clouds of the Persian Gulf.

"From the Power of Greyskull!" I hear from the television. "I AM THE POWER!" A cartoon male of mammoth physique holding a sword high above him is being infused by lightning. This is He-Man.

"All right," I say. "Go get 'em, He-Man."

There is no response from the couch.

George Bush is He-Man, I think suddenly, and then boom out, "By the Power of Greyskull!"

"Stop saying that, Daddy."

His voice is Warren Burger, former Supreme Court Justice. *Nobody makes fun of He-Man.*

Suddenly letters drop through the mail slot. I move slowly to the door. On top of the pile is a small yellow envelope. I pick it up. In the upper left-hand corner I see the return address is San Diego, the name Dawn Templeton, and my heart starts singing like a lark on the wing.

When Gardner was our only boy and deep into his backhoe/dumptruck phase, I took him twice to an abandoned backhoe which we could see from the highway on the way into Boston. It was sitting in a ruined field among dumps of broken pavement and piles of earth, like a tank after a war. The housing was dull yellow; the tracks, boom, and bucket were deep rust. On the counterweight in capitals was spelled "INSLEY." Cables were twisted in the grass nearby; Gardner named it "Alexander," after his cousin in California.

We went once in spring to explore the way, parking at the end of an industrial park and walking through several hundred yards of desolation. For some reason or other, we didn't have much time, so we looked Alexander over briefly and then left, planning to return at our leisure. The second time was midsummer, and we went to play. I helped him into the cab. There was very little glass, so I merely told him to be careful and stepped away to watch. He climbed onto the broken seat and looked out over the boom, perhaps measuring the power he imagined beneath him. Then he took hold of the levers and began to rattle them.

From where I stood, I could see a football shape beneath the cab, could see it shiver, attached to the connecting rods of the controls he was manipulating. "Stop!" I shouted, and ran toward him. "Stop!"

Even as he turned to me, he gave another tug.

Suddenly they were swarming below him, mushrooming out from under the cab and curling up like angry smoke. Truly frightened, I ran at the open door, my arms wide.

"Jump!" I yelled. "Jump!"

His face crumpled in fear; then one must have got him, for he began to scream. I felt another one slam against my cheek, faint fire compared to the heat of my terror, as he leapt over the rusty track into my arms. I raced the two of us away from the machine.

He wept for a while, but each of us was stung only once and I was able to cover both stings with mud, which salved the pain. "That was bad of Alexander," he said, his voice rich with betrayal and tears. In that moment I realized that I would do anything, go anywhere, bear any hurt at all, so that he might be safe.

Here in the Greenwich zone 4:30 P.M. is 8:30 A.M. in California's, and I punch the codes—international, U.S., southern California, the number itself—into the system, hoping that she'll be there, be awake, be cheerful.

When are stewardesses at home, I have always wondered, and what time do they get up in the mornings?

Dawn Templeton's letter explained that she'd found the briefcase and that she wanted to be sure of the proper address for returning it. She was on a flight from Bangor, Maine, to Los Angeles when she discovered it deep in an overhead compartment. We are no closer to getting it back than we were a week ago, I have realized, but after I talk with her we will be. The question of whether to wait for it or to take other steps to pick up our car in Cambridge hangs fire. We have decided that there's an advantage to learning our neighborhood on bus and foot.

The phone buzzes, clicks, and then a voice, clear as next door: "Hello?"

"Hello, Dawn Templeton?"

"Yes."

I identify myself. "I'm the idiot who left his briefcase on a plane you worked last week."

"Of course. I have it. Do you want me to send it to you?"

Words fail me. I start to stammer, pleas and promises.

"Don't worry. I'll go down to Federal Express today and send it off."

At six o'clock we are in the kitchen, having just sat down at the round shiny black table. Sam has an ancient white high chair, its tray covered with white contact paper. The tray latch is a spring-and-wire affair, probably dating from just after World War II.

"Who should say the blessing, Gardner?"

"No blessing."

This game has been going on for a time, but in England it has become invariable. Jane seeks to involve him more deeply in the blessing of the food, and he is equally determined to disengage himself from it.

"Well, then, we'll have a silent grace." She takes my hand, and I lean over to hold Sam's, which struggles toward the hamburger. Gardner will not hold hands at all; but, when after a pause with our heads bent she says, "Amen," he echoes loudly, "Amen—Gloria to the ceiling!"

She laughs. "Did you boys have a good time swimming?" Rejoicing after the Dawn Templeton call, we got Sam up from his nap and went to the public pool down the street.

"Yeah. I went into the big pool. They gave me a surfboard."

"I think it's a kickboard, really."

"That's right. A kickboard."

"So we're going to get our briefcase back?"

"Sometime. Soon, I hope."

"In time for next weekend? We want to go to Warwick Castle, and school starts in less than two weeks."

"Who knows? Maybe we should think about London for the next weekend. We'd never take a car in there. At least I wouldn't."

"I don't want to go to school."

"No?" I ask. "Gee. What would you do instead? You'd get pretty bored, wouldn't you?"

"Right," adds Jane. "Everybody else would be in school, and you'd be all by yourself."

"Gardner? Would you like to go to the Tower of London next week?"

"What's that?"

"It's very cool. It's a castle, really, not a tower, and it's where the kings and queens of England were put in prison. Some of them had their heads chopped off there."

His eyes widen slightly.

"Plus it's where they keep the crown jewels."

"Oh, yeah? Can we see them?"

"Sure can. Want to go?"

"Sure." He takes a small bite from his plate. "Mom. I don't like this hamburger."

Ever since he was an infant, we have been putting him to bed using the same routine: stories, the Lord's Prayer, and a lullabye I wrote, loosely based on the old Brahms tune:

> Lullabye, lullabye,
> Oh, my Gardie, don't you cry,
> Gardie's angels up above,
> Take care of the boy I love,
> Lullabye, and good-night,
> In your dreams I'll hold you tight;
> Lullabye, and good night,
> Till the dawn's early light.

Jane sings the melody and I have worked out some simple upper harmony. We have sung this song, duet or solo, every night when at least one of us is home for the past four years. We can sing it in our sleep. Perhaps we do.

We also give him a cup of apple juice that we have been unable to write out of the bedtime script. Still, despite—or perhaps because of—these compulsions, he gives us little trouble at night. Sam, conversely, has never slept as long or as hard as his brother. He weeps at bedtime and is up at six, while Gardner seems to require at least ten hours and sometimes twelve, luxuriating in sleep, leaving it only with reluctance. When he was younger and napping, he would sleep so hard in the afternoon that he could not easily awake; at the day-care center the teacher reported weeping or tantrums if they tried to rouse him before he was ready.

Tonight I am reading to him a chapter of *Freddy the Cowboy*, one of a series of books about a pig named Freddy and his friends Jinx the cat and Mrs. Wiggins the cow, a series I myself read and loved when I was young. Freddy has just bought a cowpony named Cy and is learning to ride.

"Dad, do they have cowboys in England?"

"No, I don't think so. They ride horseraces and have foxhunts on horseback." He knows about foxhunts from another Freddy book. "Also the knights used to ride horses. When they jousted."

"I know."

Jane comes in and we pray and sing. He is lying on his bed, his legs reflexed, pulling on his feet. His face contorts.

"I have leg cramps."

I feel his calves and thighs, which are knotted and tight. "Roll over and relax," I say, and straightening his legs, begin to massage the hard straining muscles. "Is that helping?"

"A little," he says doubtfully.

I move my fingers to the soles of his feet and knead there, watching his face intently. Gradually it loosens and his thumb finds his mouth, the bunny ear his cheek; once and yet again I have worked pain from his body. Now he is quiet, gently breathing, and I kiss his cheek just before he falls into the soft darkness he calls sleep.

5

A week has passed, and we have heard nothing about the briefcase. Every time a Federal Express truck passes my wife or me on the street—and they seem to be ubiquitous—our hearts leap to the roofs of our mouths, and we have to restrain ourselves from flagging it down. On Friday I called the nearest Fed Ex office in Kidlington, but without the particular shipping number I could not trace the location of the package. To be honest, I worry that Dawn Templeton was hit by a bus on the way to the Federal Express office in San Diego, or that she ran off with a boyfriend to Tijuana, or that her Afghan ate the bag and all its contents. Where is my faith?

Despite these doubts we have not let grass grow under our feet. I have picked two quarts of blackberries and baked pies. The flour we use is different from that at home, but I'm getting the hang of it. The berries, which are just coming into season, are pitty but tasty; I figure I can freeze them in plastic bags for pies during the winter. The embankment is loaded with them, clusters of sweet dark jewels defended by spiny branches.

I have furthermore bought a bicycle. On Wednesday I took a bus into Oxford and, after getting directions, walked down Walton Street past the Oxford University Press into the section of the city known as Jericho. At last I came to Cycle King, where I asked to see the bottom line in used machines. The hairy young clerk pointed out into the back yard, where fifty or so rusty old warriors canted crazily in line.

"You can have any of them for twenty quid. Go out and look around."

Mostly they were rough: bent wheels, broken seats, brakes and cables stripped and hanging off. One looked possible, almost fancy, until I pulled it from the line to discover it had no crankshaft. Ultimately I found a blue five-speed with blue fenders—as well as brakes, pedals, wheels, handlebars, cables, a chain, and a seat. It would need new tires sooner rather than later and oil as soon as possible, but I felt certain it would carry me the eight miles home.

On the receipt the clerk wrote: "Secondhand racer—As Seen: £20.00."

The ride between Woodstock and Oxford is pleasant, taking about forty minutes on my new secondhand racer. The terrain is mostly flat, with the wide bikepath next to the A34. As I pedal along I see the autumn flowers—wild rose, Oxford ragwort, bindweed, daisy, teasel. At one point the road rises over a canal, along the banks of which grow clumps of purple jewelweed, known here as Himalayan balsam, in splendid profusion. This plant is apparently something of a problem, despite its lovely blossoms: an Asian import, escaped from gardens, invading wet areas and choking out native species. I recall the loosestrife that turns entire marshes purple back in Massachusetts—glorious in the soft yellow light of late afternoon—as it signals doom for less aggressive flowers like cardinal flower and arrowhead.

In addition to purchasing the bicycle this week, I finished re-reading *Emma* and *Pride and Prejudice*, the latter a novel I have always particularly loved. I have only *Northanger Abbey* and the early and unfinished work to go over and I will be ready to visit Jane Austen's world—Hampshire, south of here, west of London—to see it with her words ringing in my ears. I have also gone to Mr. Taylor, the local electrician, asking him to obtain for me a transformer of some sort that will allow me to use my computer. He is confident such an article will not be impossible to find. I suspect, however, that I may require a further outlay of patience before I am on-line.

Jane has been visited by someone involved in the Movement for the Ordination of Women—"MOW: A WOMAN'S PLACE IS IN THE HOUSE—OF BISHOPS"—and is starting to hear rumbles of conferences she may be invited to participate in. This activity provides me with a subtle but perceptible relief. It is important to both of us that her presence in England be significant, both personally and professionally. She is doing lots of journal keeping and reflecting and praying, all of which are part of her plan for the year. Still, her presence in this country at this time ought to be noted, indeed be made use of, by those members of the Church of England who want an example of how good a woman priest can be. Both of us would be unhappy to see her talent buried for a year in the Hereford House garden.

One day this week we all joined Jane, Harriet, and Peter Brown by the lake in Blenheim for a picnic. We went swimming twice at the public pool. And yesterday, Friday, we all went to the Woodstock Surgery to introduce ourselves to the baseline unit of the British national health system.

"Surgery" sounds much more serious than "clinic," which is what a surgery really is. In Woodstock we find it a rich resource, supported from the budget of the Woodstock Town Council or the Oxfordshire County Council, I'm not sure which, although I know that my poll tax contributions help to pay for it: five general practitioners—Drs. Edwards, Hope, Martin, Swift, and Van Oss—working together with a support staff of nurses and aides in a building tucked off High Street on a tiny thoroughfare called Rectory Lane.

We arrived at our appointed hour and met with an intelligent, friendly nurse, who measured the boys in inches and feet and weighed them in stones and kilograms. We understood three feet one inch and four feet even, but when Gardner scaled out at twenty-five point five kilograms, and Sam two stone three, we felt confused. We didn't tell the nurse this but related with assurance their medical histories and handed over their immunization records. She smiled at us, reassured us, answered questions; and when we left, we felt secure, safe, and warm, cradled in the great bosom of the nation, of the Queen, perhaps even of Margaret Thatcher.

So the missing briefcase is the only fly in a fine sweet ointment, and today, Saturday, the first of September, we are taking the train into London. This is a great adventure for both boys. The countryside flies by, green fields dotted with cows and sheep, towns and canals and farms, unreeling at breakneck speed past the window. Suddenly on the west side of the train loom six huge cylinders.

"Wow," I say.

"What's that, Dad?"

"Right," says Jane. "England went into nuclear power without any qualms. Anything to reduce their dependence on oil."

"It's a plant to make electricity. Wow. It's pretty big, isn't it?" I feel a sudden flash of memory of Three Mile Island, of Chernobyl, but I try to keep my voice clear of it.

He looks out the window at the passing giants but says nothing more. I realize I have no idea what he is thinking.

From Paddington Station, we take the Tube to Tower Station, where Gardner and I will tour that grim castle. Jane and Sam will stroll across the city to St. James Park; there we will rendezvous at the end of the lake in front of Buckingham Palace for lunch.

The sun is bright as we pass through the turnstile and move toward a crowd gathering for the next tour. "Mom and I were here when we were in England before," I tell him. "It's very cool. Those men in the funny red costumes are called Beefeaters. I don't know why, but they may tell us. What I remember best are the ravens."

"What?"

"The ravens. Big, black birds. They keep them here at the castle."

The crowd is so large it's hard to hear. I hold him on my shoulders, all twenty-five and a half kilograms of him, as the Beefeater begins to describe some of the hangings that occurred above the castle on Tower Hill. Then he leads us through the gate. His voice is loud, spacing and emphasizing his words like missiles. "As we pass through, notice the portcullis hanging above your heads. It weighs more than a ton. It has never slipped, but, if it should and someone be hit, the concussion would doubtless tingle a great deal. Please be careful. I wouldn't want to lose any member of the tour."

It is the sort of detail that appeals to my son, but I can tell he's having trouble understanding what's being said. "Look up," I tell him as we walk under. "See that gate up there? That's called a portcullis. He said it weighs over a ton. He said he doesn't want anyone to get hurt if it falls."

"Will it fall?"

"I hope not."

After we are through, I can feel him twist to look up again. "Ha. I hope it does." He likes this power of Greyskull stuff; I can imagine his grin.

After a time I set him back on the ground. He can't attend to the tales of horror the Beefeater is relishing, but he's looking around with interest, walking through the legs of the crowd, being independent. On a long flight of steps, the sun slanting past the towers, the Beefeater stops and points out some ravens on a lawn below us. The boy is some distance from me, but I think he is listening to the birds' story, that should they ever leave, the crown of England would fall. The harsh, carefully spaced words continue:

"Last year, for the first time in history, a raven egg was hatched here in the Tower. A contest was held by the BBC among all the children in Great Britain to give the little fellow a name. I regret to tell you that the winning name was Ronald Raven."

The adults roar; the children, my son among them, gaze blankly down at the birds. Then we proceed up to the site of Anne Boleyn's execution. He is clearly growing bored, despite my attempts to reinterpret the Beefeater's tale. Suddenly he spots a small group of guardsmen—scarlet tunics, black furry helmets, shouldered rifles—marching across the courtyard to relieve one of their number. The sight freezes him, his jaw drops slightly.

"Check out those guys," I say into his ear.

"What are they?"

"They're the guards. See the one on duty? He's not allowed to *move*. Not a muscle. After they relieve him, he can go rest, while another guard has to stand there like a statue."

Intently he watches the change of guard. "Are their guns real?"

"Oh, sure. I would think so. Wouldn't you?"

We watch the new guard for nearly five minutes after the others have marched away. Sure enough, he stands still as a pillar in the warm sun, though I can see his lip wrinkle when a bead of sweat rolls across it.

"What if they have to go to the bathroom?"

"I guess they just have to tough it out. They probably make sure to go right before they come on duty."

Gardner has revived. We wait patiently in the long line passing by the royal silver, the robes, and deep in the vaults below, the Crown Jewels. He is impressed. Then we climb up to the armory to see the old weapons—swords, crossbows, knives, firearms, and great suits of armor, including the one worn by the six-wived, barrel-bodied sovereign who made so much use of the facilities here, Henry VIII. Gardner is growing tired, I can tell, despite the wonders before his eyes, so we push into the gift shop, which contains sterling-silver models of the Tower for hundreds of pounds, jewelry and glassware and books and dishtowels and postcards—and a bin of small painted models of knights for fifty pence each.

He spends ten minutes turning the bin's contents through his hands, lining them on the edge of the counter. "Dad, which one do you like best?"

"You can buy two, you know."

"I know that." This is his Peter Jennings "World News To-night" voice. Two is enough. He is in one of his happiest moods, utterly focused, reveling in his choices, certain that he can make them without leaving an unchosen treasure behind.

"Well, I like the guy with the spear."

It is often difficult to understand the motives of children. Standing as they do so close to the borders of language—some, like Sam, not even across yet, others seemingly in the country yet nonetheless linguistically unreliable—they seldom say precisely what they mean. Often they turn instead to subverbal expression, which has an advantage in that it never lies, but a concomitant drawback in that it is sometimes ambiguous or at least hard to interpret. So I cannot be sure if I am being complimented, but I feel a stab of pleasure when he says, "I like that guy, too. I want him and the knight on the horse."

We meet the other two in St. James Park, where Sam is terrorizing the ducks and the pigeons, and find an outdoor food kiosk. One of the choices on the menu being hot dogs, we decide to test yet another translation of America to England. I muse on the Ninja Turtles becoming Heroes over here. What have our hero sandwiches become?— surely not ninjas. I watch the vendor, a young black man, drive what I might call a dinner roll onto a fat aluminum spike, boring a long hole through it. Then in a distinctly Freudian gesture he forces a hot dog into the roll.

It looks good, but it isn't. The roll is stale, the hot dog soft and mushy. It is true, as I told Jane Brown, that when I was in graduate school I began a collection of recipes that was published as *The Great Little Hot Dog Cookbook*. I do not mean to suggest that I am a connoisseur of hot dogs, nor that even such a connoisseurship would be valuable or necessary—only that I have eaten and enjoyed hot dogs over a long period of time, with and without baseball games in front of them, and the example I have just bought here in St. James Park is the worst I have ever put in my mouth. It tastes as if it has come out of a tin can, reminding me of small horrors called Viennese sausages, a can of which I one time bought in all innocence while in graduate school. I begin to understand that the real danger of being American in England may not be the subtle shiftings of language—Ninja to Hero, for instance—but those of reality—hot dog to hot dog.

The boys play in a small playground until it's time to head back to Paddington, to Oxford, to Woodstock. That night Gardner sets his two knights on the shelf above his bed. I read to him a retelling of the first book of *The Faerie Queen,* gloriously illustrated, titled *St. George and the Dragon.* He has heard this story many times and loves it still: Una and the dwarf, the vision of the Celestial City, the huge roaring dragon with its brassy scales, sharp claws, and fiery breath. We read the entire book while Jane is putting Sam to bed.

"There," I say. "A rough life being a knight, eh?"

He doesn't answer, only smiles, and then Jane comes in for prayers and lullabies. Afterward we sit in the living room, I continuing Jane Austen, she working in her journal. In *Northanger Abbey* Catherine Morland is learning, like Emma Woodhouse and Elizabeth Bennet, that she has allowed her preconceptions to overrule her good sense, although she has a sweeter disposition than either of them. Henry Tilney, who recognizes her virtues as well as her shortcomings, says to her, "You feel, as you always do, what is most to the credit of human nature—Such feelings ought to be investigated, that they may know themselves."

I share this desire with Catherine Morland, to feel what is most to the credit of human nature. My sons are sleeping upstairs, dreaming of ducks and pigeons or knights and dragons. My wife and I are reading and writing below, feeling productive and content. Perhaps I sense subconsciously that the investigation of such happiness might impair it; in any case I do not apply the second half of Tilney's remark to myself.

6

*T*omorrow — Wednesday, September 3—school starts. Although it's hard to read the Young Scholar's feelings, my wife and I are enthusiastic about the prospect. Not a kindergarten exactly: for the first year the children will be mixed vertically by age, with five-, six-, and seven-year-olds blended together in an olio of enthusiasm and noise.

We are intrigued by the vertical arrangement of the lowest class. This is an experiment in Woodstock, instigated by the principal, who like our son has newly arrived here. It is, incidentally, the precise opposite of the school he would be attending back home. There all the kindergartners in town have been put into a single school building, an "Early Learning Center," with regular classes and testing facilities and special "readiness" groups. We can see the advantages to this approach, especially for children with developmental glitches; but Gardner has always seemed bright, though perhaps a bit cautious intellectually, unwilling to take a risk if he fears he might fail. Still, he is often attracted to children older than he—as, for instance, his "friends" in the neighborhood—so we think he may find a niche in a class with older students, and so become happier.

Jane walked over to an orientation session yesterday and brought back a positive picture. She met Mrs. Tattam, his teacher, who seemed pleasant and competent. "It's a nice classroom," she reported. "There are lots of materials there—even a computer for the children to play with. He should love it."

The Woodstock C. of E. Primary School itself is, by my standards, quite new, the building maybe twenty years old, a single story brick-and-glass structure that could quite easily be standing in Woodstock, Georgia, or any of the Woodstocks in Illinois, Maryland, New York, and Vermont. The main difference is the "C. of E."—Church of England—business, indicating that it was founded by the established church. A number of primary schools in England—though by no means all—bear this designation, which sounds to my ear like the term "parochial school" in America. It's not, though. C. of E. primary schools now no longer have formal ecclesiastical ties, no long have a rector hiring and firing teachers and pupils like the tyrannical Rev. Brocklehurst in *Jane Eyre,* although the school year maintains a close relationship with the church calendar. Later this fall the children will walk down to St. Mary Magdalene's for a Harvest Festival. There will be a Christmas pageant. More regularly, hymn singing happens. Other than these vestiges of antidisestablishmentarianism (how many years have I waited to be able to write this word, which in my own primary school we believed the longest in English?) it seems quite familiar, and we feel ourselves blessed with a broad, rich pedagogical mix, with lots of challenges for Gardner.

Furthermore, we discovered that Peter Brown—who is still the only boy he knows—will be in Mrs. Tattam's class. Wonderful, we said.

Another event occurred while Jane was visiting the school. At the second post a letter from Federal Express fell through the slot.

To review, we arrived on August 13 and lost the briefcase; I called Dawn Templeton on August 24; and after several telephone queries I heard from Federal Express yesterday, September 3. With fingers trembling with joy—no exaggeration—I opened the letter. It contained a customs form. The briefcase is at the Birmingham International Airport, awaiting clearance.

There is nothing to declare in the briefcase. It contains only papers, photographs, and a set of car keys. I was on the phone in an instant to Federal Express's toll-free exchange:

"What is the consignment number, sir?" asked a woman.

I read it from the slip, feeling as I did so the vibrations of her tapping into her computer.

"It's in customs right now, awaiting clearance."

"I know that." I gritted my teeth. "Can I speed up the process?"

"I don't know, sir. Perhaps if you call our Birmingham office."

Of course I called the Birmingham office. "Suppose I take a train up to the airport. Could that speed things up? We are very anxious to get our car, you see."

"Well, the customs people are difficult to hurry along."

"It has been there for more than two weeks."

"I'm sorry, sir. We can't do anything until you fill in that form. Send it right out, and in a day or so we should have it through."

So I filled out the form and, as soon as Jane got home, cycled it straight to the post office. What else could I do?

Today we plan to celebrate the final day of vacation by going to the St. Giles Fair in Oxford. We take the 3:10 bus, which, because of the fair, detours along

Walton Street as we approach the city center. "Look," I say, pointing. "That's where I bought my bicycle."

The St. Giles Fair is famous—notorious, even—in England. Supposedly one autumn during World War II the authorities decided to cancel it because of the risk of gathering too many people in one place, but the public outcry was so great that the show went on anyway. We have no idea what to expect. I grew up in Maine with county fairs every fall, so I'm ready for everything from horse pulls to pumpkin judging to strip shows.

One of the main streets in Oxford has at least four names. Down by the River Thames it's called St. Aldates, at the center it's Cornmarket—where we had our alien photos taken—then for a block it becomes Magdalene. Finally at the Martyrs' Monument, before it splits into the Woodstock Road and the Banbury Road, it widens into St. Giles Street. Here, naturally enough, we discover the fair.

It is a midway, a mini–Atlantic City Boardwalk, with loop-the-loops and fun houses and cotton-candy stands and slides and ring toss and darts and bumper cars. Both boys are transported, their mouths slackjawed, their eyes rolling down their cheeks.

"Why don't I take Sam and you take Gardie?" suggests Jane.

We have twenty pounds. "Here," I say. "You guys take five, and we'll take five. After we've spent them all, we'll regroup here by the monument for supper."

Gardner and I begin to wander, or rather he does, and I follow him. He walks up on the balls of his feet, bouncing slightly, his head cocking to first one side and then the other. He looks hard at a dart booth and then across the way sees a set of bumper cars, the real thing, just like I used to drive when I was twelve at Old Orchard Beach in Maine.

I've never been able to figure out how bumper cars work. I can see that they are powered by electricity, like trolley cars with their booms scraping against the sparking chicken-wire ceiling; but I have never understood how they steer: one cranks that wheel around while they sit there immobile until suddenly they lurch into some direction or other, often the opposite of what is expected. Equally surprising is their stability as they take slams from any direction. They are at once ungainly and iron steady. I'd love to see the bottom of one someday, to discover what configuration of wheels creates such loco-motion.

As a child I loved them, and my son is likewise taken. His eyes are burning with excitement. They are real, after all, real cars that one must steer and drive. "Dad. I want to drive on the bumper cars."

"Sure. Do you want to go with me?" I wonder about giving him this choice, for he probably won't be able to steer very well. On the other hand, he won't get hurt.

"Can I drive by myself?"

"Sure." It costs ninety pence. During a lull in the bumping he runs onto the floor and climbs into a bright blue machine.

"Hold on tight!" shouts the attendant, and they begin to swirl and bang away at each other. At first I am for some reason taken aback by the collective motion, which has a foreign look to it, until I realize that they are going clockwise. At Old Orchard Beach, even as children we were ingrained with driving on the right and always tended to maintain a counterclockwise motion. Here of course they keep to the left.

Out on the floor Gardner is having difficulty. He has no idea how to direct the car, nor even where it should go. A huge clot of traffic has been created with him at the center. The point of bumper cars being that they should be free to move in order to bump, the other drivers are growing frustrated at this logjam. I feel a wave of helpless pity for him, and then the attendant steps fearlessly from bumper to bumper to crouch over him, to steer him out and around and even into one or two cars. At last the ride is over.

"How was that?"

"O.K." He seems somewhat crestfallen, however, and regret stabs me. I did not want any part of this day even to hint at failure.

"They are tough to steer, I know."

We continue walking. He looks longingly at a fun house, but says nothing. Just beside it is a small carousel of eight cars, two of them resembling the Batmobile, a ride his younger brother would love. It is to bumper cars what bumper cars are to the Daytona 500.

"I want to go on that."

"Sure."

He rides around happily in the Batmobile, his pride and self-confidence gradually rebuilding. He has always been like this, an ego both demanding and fragile, which desperately needs success—any success to repair its punctures.

Afterward he asks, "Can I go in the fun house now?"

"You want to?"

"Yes."

"O.K. I want to come, too." I don't, of course, but the importance of this trip is manifest. The fun house is actually a trailer, with a facade that unfolds and opens out; inside are narrow walls and stairs and passageways folding around each other. It is an old one; every now and then through a gap in a curtain or corner, a cluster of the air hoses that move the parts and hiss at the patrons is visible, like a family of snakes. And so I stumble after him through the dark chambers of horror, over the sliding floors, up the moving stairs, over the hanging bridge, clear to the end.

"That was neat!"

We keep moving. At one stand I throw enough balls to win him a poster of the Teenage Mutant Hero Turtles. We look at The Rocket, a truly frightening ride, and decide not to try it. We pass sausage stands and ice cream vendors. Eventually we stand looking up at a tall yellow tower from which issues a spiraling slide.

"I want to do this one."

"Oh, no. Really?"

"Sure." He is fully cocked now, laughing at me as I parody nervousness.

"It's pretty darn high."

"Come *on*, Dad."

We are given rough cotton smocks and a hemp mat. He begins climbing the stairs, and I follow. The tower is perhaps twenty feet, with crenellations at the top. By the time we reach it, I am puffing, so we pause to look over St. Giles Street, teeming below us like a Breughel painting.

Then we arrange ourselves on the mat, my son seated on my lap, and with a push we are away: like a song my barbershop quartet used to sing, "Down and down I go, round and round I go, like a leaf caught in the tide." Much of that song is written in iambic pentameter, and for a joke I have sung in place of "That old black magic has me in its spell" Yeats's spinning words: "Turning and turning in the widening gyre / The falcon cannot hear the falconer." And so we are swept, down to the street, cries of excited joy breaking from both our throats, together.

On the first day of school the whole family goes, Gardner bouncing along first ahead of, then behind, Sam in his stroller. It is a two-minute walk, just two buildings away. The sky is cloudy, and the children are swarming about the doors in yellow and red and blue raincoats. There is a large area of tarmac here with game patterns painted down: hopscotch, ladders, basketball, a crude map of the world. On the other side of the building is a larger field of grass, level and closely trimmed, a fine football pitch.

Inside we find the classroom brightly lit despite the outside gray, filled with children and parents, who beetle from one station to the next, dropping off coats and wellies, examining pencil cases and artwork, chatting with friends and the teacher. I go over to the book corner with Gardner, who looks over with me and without enthusiasm the titles in the library.

"Hullo, you," speaks a laconic voice.

Gardner continues to inspect one of the books.

"Hello, Peter Brown," I say, looking up. "How are you this morning?"

"Fine." He sees what is in our hands, a beginning reader containing pictures and the words, "I," "am," "coming," "here," "going," "there," and suddenly on the last page, "not."

"I know that book."

"Do you?" I say.

"Yeah. I read it last year." Peter, having turned five eight months ago, started school the previous January.

"Really? Can you still?" Innocently curious, I hand it to him.

" 'I am coming.' " He turns the page. " 'I am coming here.' "

I look down at Gardner. He stares at Peter intently, all expression clear of his face, holding his breath. Without moving my own eyes I say, "That's good, Pete. That's just right." My son's mouth grows rigid and set, but still there is no describable expression, only hardening concrete, a face at last as blank as a sidewalk.

That afternoon, however, school seems to have gone well enough. I don't ask any questions, but both he and Peter—who comes home with him to play—seem energized by their day. Later at supper, though, he is not hungry. "My stomach is cramped."

"You should eat something," Jane says. "Don't you like this spaghetti? You asked for it, remember?"

He takes a microscopic bite. "I don't like it."

Jane and I look at each other, and she compresses her lips. "Well, you have to eat something. How about a peanut butter and jelly sandwich?"

"O.K."

He bites away at it tentatively. With his bottom teeth covered by his lip, the top set cutting partway through the bread, he tears small fragments from the whole. He has a loose lower incisor, so this may be a defensive eating posture, I can't be sure. When he masticates, his mouth stays lightly open and he seems to be chewing with his tongue and the roof of his mouth, as if he is trying to abandon the use of his teeth.

"How was school?" I try.

He tears away another bit of his sandwich and looks at his plate.

"More," says Sam.

"I'm glad somebody likes this ghetti," says Jane. She scrapes Gardner's refused portion onto the high chair tray. "Tell Daddy about your book."

He begins to hum, which is not one of his voices exactly, but which means, "No Torture Will Make Me Talk."

"We have a reading book," she explains. "He reads it to us, instead of the other way around."

"No," I say. "Does this mean I don't get to read stories to you any more?"

He looks up coldly. "No."

The book proves to be another in the basal series from which Peter Brown read successfully that morning: "Look! I See!" Whimsical illustrations portray a small person being shown a series of surprising sights by a friend. A curveball comes flying off the final pages, where the tables are turned, the friend the one who is surprised: "Look! You see!"

Gardner—who can recite a number of favorite stories without missing a word—quickly falls into the rhythm of "Look!"—page turn—"I see!" He is fooled, however, by the last page.

"Look! I see!"

"Oops," I say, pointing to the *Y* in "You." "What's that letter?"

He looks at me in surprise. "I don't know."

On Friday on the way to school with Jane he trips and weeps violently, clinging desperately when she tries to leave him. "Oh, Lord," I say when she gets back. "You know, he doesn't know the alphabet to the end."

"He doesn't know it at all. Remember, they told us at day care he was resisting learning it?"

"I thought *Sesame Street* was supposed to fix that. Poor guy. This may not be easy for him."

"He doesn't know it at all."

That afternoon after school they walk to town to Vanbrugh's Cake Shop—named in honor of the builder of Blenheim Palace—for tea. When they return, Sam and I are kicking a small ball around the garden.

"How did it go?" I ask ambiguously enough.

He says nothing, only goes to the Quadro structure and begins to climb.

"We had a nice tea," says Jane.

"I called Federal Express."

"Oh? What did they say?"

"Apparently I made a mistake on the form. I didn't check one of the boxes."

"Oh, no."

"I have to fill out a new form."

"Oh, no."

"Oh, shit."

At night Gardner cries bitterly, complaining of severe stomach cramps. We take his temperature to find it normal. He is up several times to pee, or to complain of leg cramps. About four o'clock in the morning he vomits in his bed, in the hall, and all over the bathroom. After everything is cleaned up, he comes to bed with his mother, while I go to his bed to sleep what is left of the night. Even when he was a baby, he rarely threw up, and this is only the second time he has done so in the last four years.

7

*T*his Sunday I am riding in a motor coach, resting on dark blue cushions. From outside the window the Midlands unreel, green to brown to green, flat to rolling to flat, country to town to country. The sun, which has slowly risen off the east-southeast horizon, has grown bright yellow and is beginning to whiten. The passing fields are dotted with sheep and cows, ghostly in the morning mist.

Early this morning Martyn Brown drove me into Oxford to the bus station, where I took the first coach to Cambridge to retrieve the car we bought from my colleague. This fact does not mean the briefcase has been restored; it has not. On Friday morning, when it did not arrive and Federal Express told me it had not yet cleared customs, I turned to Jane. "Fuck," I said, and she did not remonstrate. On Friday afternoon, exasperated beyond measure at the lack of car keys and papers and the knowledge of where the car is parked, I called its former owner back in the States and got the name and address of the couple who have been watching it and who have been keeping an extra set of keys. Then

I called them, arranging that they be home to greet me when I arrive this morning.

It is a judgment on me, a measure of one of my defects of character, that I have taken so long to act about this car. I have let so much energy, psychic and otherwise, be consumed by the Briefcase Affair that I have simply been unable to put myself into motion. Partly it's because I am a person who likes to perform tasks in order, to solve one problem before moving on to the next, to finish the brussels sprouts before beginning the candied yams.

When I called Don Barry, my colleague, about the car, I discovered another consequence of my procrastination. "It's, let's see, the seventh today," he said. "I'm afraid that means that both the insurance and the license have run out. I thought sure you'd pick up the car before now."

"So did I." I paused, then blew a puff of air. "What the hell. In for a penny, in for a pound, as we say here."

He laughed. "You won't have any trouble."

"Right," I said.

One other person, a young man with a mustache, is on the coach with me. After helping each other make change, we chatted a bit before boarding, but now we are sitting apart. I want to look out upon this country and see it; I want also to prepare my mind for the horrifying prospect of driving back to Woodstock. My road map is spread in the seat beside me so I may consider the route we are taking and those I may choose in return. I am terrified about driving on the left side of the road. This is probably another reason why I have put off collecting the car so long. Like a baseball player imagining bat contact in the on-deck circle, I gaze out the window and visualize myself speeding down this road, this A43, at this instant coming into this roundabout with jaunty confidence; and I shiver.

Outside Luton the coach passes a huge field bristling with

maybe thirty electronic towers. I am astonished; this is a country with four television stations and not many more radio ones. What on earth do they do with all those towers? I wonder. We wind down into Luton itself—the name sounding musical in my ears, with its echoes of "lute"—in actuality a homely center of agriculture and industry, sleeping this morning but doubtless busy enough during the week. The coach swings underneath a large new building and stops in a bay, beyond which I can see the ticket office. Luton is the destination of my fellow passenger. I wonder what brings him from Oxford to this place so early on a Sunday morning—not worship, surely, nor occupation; perhaps love or recreation? A new car? I wave good-bye to him as he rises from his seat. A woman climbs on and begins to chat up the driver. Although she knows him, she seems to be neither coworker nor passenger. Maybe she is a groupie of the coach drivers' union.

When the coach gets back on the road, I find myself the sole rider. "They'd have done better," I tell myself, "to hire a van." No such thing: the nationalized public transportation system has no need to cut corners in such an undignified fashion. Grateful astonishment makes me blink, for I see I am being carried like a feather to Cambridge, not so much on the upholstered seat of this coach, but on the very lap of this nation.

The fields grow flatter. They are all surrounded by hedgerows or high stone walls or fences. They are all under cultivation or pasture. There are few trees. I keep looking for woods, for unused hardscrabble, for wasteland, but these scarcely exist here. All land is enclosed, virtually every square yard is used for something. I have noticed this in Woodstock, where the only wild-looking land is behind the walls of the Blenheim Palace grounds, but today I am seeing it again, anew—that even in this flat, uninteresting, unbeautiful section of the country, all the land has been claimed and reclaimed, used and reused.

So I turn away from the window and the passing Midlands to pick up a book. I have finished Jane Austen's novels, including the early *Lady Susan* and the unfinished *Sanditon* and *The Watsons*. As further impetus to pick up the car, a trip to Hampshire has been planned, so I may visit the sites of her life and death, which seem to have shaped her writing. The Bennets' Meryton and Emma's Hartfield have the ring of her home, of Steventon and Deane, and I want to see what they look like. One of my purposes here in England is to refine my literary imagination by setting it against the actual world the literature was composed in and was supposed to reflect, insofar as that world exists today. I hope Hampshire doesn't look like what's passing by outside my window now.

Having completed Austen's works, I am taking up the seventeen novels of Thomas Hardy. I know some of them well, especially *The Mayor of Casterbridge*, which I've taught several times, but there are many I've never heard of before. This is a good year to study Hardy; 1990 is his one hundred and fiftieth birthday, and celebrations are going off all over the country. A stamp has been issued in his honor. In a couple of weeks a play called *Wessex Days*, based on his work, is being presented in Chipping Norton, eight miles north of Woodstock, and I am hopeful we can go. I have begun with a complete stranger, *Two on a Tower*, which has developed into a love story between a married woman named Lady Viviette Constantine and a youth named Swithin St. Cleeves, a clergyman's son and an amateur astronomer. These names alone jerk me out of Jane Austen's mannered English Hampshire filled with Elizabeths and Emmas and Frank Churchills and Messrs. Knightly. Furthermore, as Hardy's plot spins toward bigamy and adultery and illicit pregnancy (Lady Constantine's brutish husband is not dead, after all), I am carried with it relentlessly toward the twentieth century and the growing sexual explicitness in its comedies and tragedies. While Jane Austen moves so easily and surely within the social and literary limitations of her age, Hardy is chafing violently at the strictures of his.

At last the coach begins to work its way into Cambridge, my stomach knotting tighter at the prospect of working my way out alone, inexperienced, illegal. It is just after 10:30 when we slide into a parking place right beside a tree-filled park, and I step down into warm sunshine. My first stop is the public toilet. (I am learning not to say "rest room" or, even worse, "bathroom." One citizen I approached last week in Oxford with that request started to laugh: "You want to take a bath, mate? Over here we do that at home. But the loo is over there.")

In the briefcase in Birmingham is a map of Cambridge with the address marked. I ask a cab driver for directions. "Which way should I walk for Kimberley Street?"

"There is no Kimberley Street in Cambridge."

"No?" I fumble for the slip of paper in my pocket.

"There's a Kimberley Road. Head that way." He points.

I walk along the park until I see a roundabout ahead. Another cab is idling by the side of the road, so I ask again and this time am given careful directions: straight ahead, across the Cam River (the Cam Bridge, Cambridge, I get it), two blocks then right, three blocks then right again. Without further difficulty I find Kimberley Road, with its tightly packed brick houses running toward the river, and then I find our car parked in front of number twenty-four.

A 1976 Austin Maxi, saloon (hatchback) body, faded red paint, registration NEB879R: this is the vehicle I bought from Don Barry last spring. He was finishing up his year here in Cambridge and knew he had an aging but serviceable creature to pass on for someone else's sabbatical. The little round tag on the passenger's side has an "8" on it, signifying that it should have been replaced last month. Perhaps this lapse will not be noticed as I roll cautiously—oh, so cautiously!—across the Midlands this afternoon.

On the other side of the street the door of 23 Kimberley opens to my ring. Mrs. Mansfield, Don's former neighbor, invites me in. She is attractive, gray-haired, smiling. "Come in. My husband is just out back. Will you have a cup of tea or coffee?" She leads me into the kitchen. "How are the Barrys?" A plate of cookies appears.

As we talk, Mr. Mansfield comes in and I am introduced. "I hope you can get it going. I went out last night. The battery is still charged, but I couldn't start it. Are you anything of a mechanic?"

The knots in my stomach hum, growing tighter still. I can change a tire or a spark plug, but waters close over my head quite quickly after that. I slug down the coffee. "Maybe we'd better try it out."

He gets the keys and we cross the street. Fooled by instinct, I walk to the passenger's side, then realize that the steering wheel is on the right and walk around the car again. I open the door and get inside. Remembering that Don told me the car has a manual choke, I pull a knob, turn the key, flutter the accelerator, and by God there is a cough and a fire and the car is running, thank Jesus! "Hey. It's working just fine."

"I didn't know it had a choke," says Mr. Mansfield.

He offers to guide me to the highway. Beside me in the car he speaks quietly, reminding me of an examining officer at a driver's test: "Turn left here at this street and left again up here." Shifting with the left hand is awkward, the gearshift itself naturally balky, but I struggle to get the hang of it. We come to a roundabout, the first I have ever been asked to negotiate in an automobile. "Just remember, always give way to the right. There, that wasn't so dreadful. That's all there is to it, and you'll do fine. This road will take you out toward Bedford. Pull over here and you can drop me at this bus stop."

"I can't thank you enough."

"Not at all. I hope you have a wonderful year in Oxford."

And I am away, my heart in my throat, staring for the route numbers I have written on a sheet of paper, A45, A428, A421, and so on, all of them sounding alike, and the sun is shining brightly, and I am driving, driving. It's like the day I got my driver's license in Maine when I was sixteen; I drove a friend named David Millay from Brunswick High School all the way to his farm in Bowdoinham, putting on thirty-five or forty unauthorized miles to test out the old 1955 Chevrolet as a solo vehicle, and all the way freedom danced within my heart and before my eyes in the shimmering roadway just beyond the hood. The rest of the family, especially Gardner, will rejoice with me in the arrival of our car.

Because of Gardner's illness on Friday night we postponed a vague plan to travel by train to Bristol, to a Lego exhibition that he is certain to like. When I get more experience on these roads—and when the car is legal—we can all drive there.

I have to stop for petrol. Prices being quoted in pounds and pence, amounts measured in liters and imperial gallons, I have absolutely no idea how much it costs here, nor even how much I'm getting for the price. Petrol is running between 43p and 45p per liter, and a penny is a bit less than two cents and a liter is a bit larger than a quart. For me to make a conversion to dollars per gallon is out of the question. I do know it's expensive by American standards, and the crisis in the Persian Gulf has levered it up further.

Driving into the station, I go the wrong way around the entrance island, but no one is coming, thank God, and I pull up to the pumps and serve myself. The fillup costs £18.00, more than

$35.00. It ain't hay, as my grandfather used to observe. I can understand it now.

The motorway was recommended to me as a longer but easier way for a rookie to drive: the M11 toward London, the M25 beltway, the M40 out to Oxford, three big superhighways without roundabouts and traffic lights. I'm glad now I have decided on the overland route instead. I pull off at a pub, where I recklessly order a half-pint of bitter and a steak and kidney pie. In English novels characters often have this combination for lunch. I find the former excellent, the latter sharp with the rich, smoky, oily taste of animal organs that I always believe I ought to like, but so seldom do.

Afterward the landscape begins to unflatten a bit and trees and leas appear more commonly. At the end of Shipton Road that tees into the A4095 I turn right across the oncoming traffic—will this act ever feel natural?—and in a couple of minutes pass the swimming pool, the secondary school, the Browns' house, the Woodstock C. of E. Primary School, the convenience store, after which I pull into a spot across from Hereford House, and I am home. Jane is waving to me over the fence.

"How did it all go today?" I ask, sitting on the couch, the house quiet, the boys in bed. "The invalid looks much improved." Gardner played at Pete Brown's, where he was invited to supper. The three of us dined on apples from the Browns' tree—Waldorf salad and apple crisp.

"It went great. We didn't go to church." I nod with complete understanding. Last week they took a cab to Wootton, three miles away, to try out the church there, while I went on a nature walk on the Blenheim grounds. Wootton seemed to her much more attentive to family worship, but the cab fare was £3.50 each way.

"So we went to Blenheim to ride on the little train and play in the playground. They were good. And I think he had a fine time this afternoon with Pete."

On television we watch, of all things, American football, the Cowboys and the Giants, edited so the game takes only sixty minutes to show. It is nine o'clock here and thus four in New York; the contest has not been over more than an hour or so, and yet here it is, flashed to us with bewildering speed. The editing dizzies me. No sooner is one ballcarrier flopping on the ground than he's up and knifing at the line once more. One does not always recognize how important rhythm is to a sport, how necessary the time in the huddle or between pitches is to prepare oneself for the possibility of the next touchdown or home run. So much of the joy of watching games is anticipation and suspense. But there is none of either here, especially with the sappy English commentator talking over the dialogue of Frank Gifford or Al Michaels or whoever it is. Jane—who grew up in Washington, D.C., and who has thus followed the Redskins nearly from her birth—agrees. "I don't care much for this. It just doesn't seem like football."

So we put on the VCR *Witness for the Prosecution,* which we taped a few days ago. It too fails to interest me, so I pick up *Two on a Tower,* while beside me Jane continues to watch the black-and-white courtroom drama. And later, when we go to bed, we are still cheerful in the small victory of having our car.

8

*T*hree items are necessary for a car to appear legally on English roads: insurance, an inspection (called an MOT), and the £100 license disk. Taking shape in my understanding is a real respect for the slow, stately, even lethargic fashion in which bureaucracy sails along in this country. I begin telephoning bright and early Monday morning to assemble the three.

I begin with AA, the British version of AAA, to which I belong. "I'd like to purchase some insurance for a car I've just bought. I'm from the States."

The woman on the other end of the line is utterly without interest. "I'll take your name, sir, and an agent will contact you."

"Um, how soon will that be?"

"As soon as possible, sir."

"In an hour? Or in a day or two? Next week?" I am keeping my voice as polite and self-effacing as that of Graham Gooch, the champion cricketer's, who on the interviews is a model of modesty.

"I couldn't say, precisely. As soon as possible."

I thank her and hang up. I know how soon that is. The first auto insurance company in the yellow pages of the telephone book is, logically enough, A-Plan Insurance. I ring them up, and a young man takes all the information about the Maxi with great cheerfulness. "What year is it?"

"It says 1976 here," I say, looking at one of the papers from the glove compartment.

"It's an 'R' series, right?"

"What?"

"Sorry. The last letter of the registration figure. The letter 'R' was used in 1977."

"Oh. So that's how the numbers work."

"Right. This year is 'G,' and now they put it at the front of the figure. They don't use a few letters, for some reason. But each year the letter is increased."

Now, when I drive, I will be looking out for "Q's" and "P's"—seeing if there are any cars on the road older than ours. He invites me to pick up the policy tomorrow in Oxford. It will cost £112.70. I can't believe that something, anything in this country, is that easy.

The door swings open, Jane and Sam back from the trip to the Woodstock Primary School. Her face tells the tale.

"He wept, eh?"

"I just don't know what to do. Mrs. Tattam says he's happy after we leave."

During the afternoons while Gardner is at school, Sam napping, and I reading, Jane creeps upstairs to the guest room to meditate and pray. There's no pressure on this room yet. Although it's where we will keep the computer, Mr. Taylor, the electrician, has still not yet pulled together the device that will make British electrical current palatable to our

Apple IIe. So for now the top floor makes a convenient, secluded chapel.

Before I married a future priest, I thought little about prayer, having mostly stopped attending church. If any thought was given the phenomenon, it concluded that prayer didn't seem to work. Petitioning the Creator to grant favors need not fail often before the petitioner turns cynical; as a child I quickly gave up praying for things. Later it seemed that people prayed to be given strength to perform some overwhelming feat or other. Perhaps Washington prayed before going out to defeat Cornwallis at Yorktown—indeed, he probably did, and prayed hard. But what of Cornwallis? Did he not pray, or if so, not hard enough?

What I believe now is that prayer is a sort of conversation, often with questions and answers, and if any request be made of Creator, Redeemer, or Sustainer, it is made with the knowledge that it may be denied, that there are no guarantees. The important gift is grace that the petitioner may understand and accept the denial. Once in a while the prayer asks for endurance. I remember Mama Younger in *A Raisin in the Sun*: "Lord, gimme strength."

Jane is reading biblical texts—she has spoken recently of the story of the sisters, Mary and Martha, Mary who rebels against everyone to sit at Jesus' feet, Martha who tries to pull her back to the kitchen where she belongs to help wash the dishes. Jane has much of Martha in her, a strong sense of duty (although she hates to wash dishes, and I have cleaned up almost every meal of our married life); upstairs in the guest room she is working this year to become more of a Mary, to hush the din of duty and sit at the feet of Christ, to listen, to understand, to accept.

Last week I read that the British Postal Service issued a set of Jane Austen stamps in honor of her bicentennial. They might be interesting to see, useful even to own, they and whatever other literary stamps England has issued, including the current Thomas Hardy commemorative. Before stopping in at A-Plan Insurance, I bicycle across Magdalene Bridge and out Cowley Road where I find a stamp and coin shop. Stamps shrink-wrapped into thick and thin packages are pinned to the walls, and used paperbacks fill racks and shelves in the back. Coins are set inside a sort of island of glass cases that fills most of the interior of the shop, in the center of which sits a dark-haired, unshaven man. He nods shyly at me, but says nothing.

"Good day," I tell him.

The proprietor's reserve continues as I explain I'm interested in literary stamps of England, including the Austen set that I understand was issued in 1975. He roots through a desk piled high with paper and books, finally extracting and thumbing through a book stuffed with packets of stamps.

There are four in the issue, white with delicately colored illustrations of various Austen characters: Emma and Mr. Woodhouse, Catherine Morland, Mr. Darcy, and Mary and Henry Crawford. He also shows me the Shakespeare four-hundredth birthday issue, a first-day cover of the Hardy commemorative, and three literary giants honored in 1971—John Keats, Thomas Gray, and Walter Scott. "That's all, as far as I know," the proprietor says mournfully.

"I'm surprised." Actually, I'm shocked. I collected stamps when I was a boy, gathering pages and pages of commemoratives in my album. The U.S. Postal Service commemorates everybody, writers, inventors, architects, doctors, lawyers, Indian chiefs I've never heard of. How can there not be stamps to commemorate Geoffrey Chaucer, Edmund Spenser, Christopher Marlowe, Samuel Johnson, William Wordsworth, Percy Bysshe Shelley, the Brontës, Virginia Woolf?

So I buy the lot. It comes to less than five pounds for the

stamps and holders to display them. This fact saddens me a bit, though I don't believe it explains the faintly melancholic air of the stamp man himself, who returns a faint "Good-bye" as I leave the shop.

A block closer to town I stop at a store called Artemis Books and lean my bicycle against the window. As I enter, the proprietress, middle-aged and gray-haired and severe as a schoolteacher, looks up from a book. "Excuse me. Would you mind moving your bicycle from the window?"

"Certainly." I hurry outside to balance it against a lightpost; not surprisingly given its origins it lacks a kickstand.

Back inside I start to look through books, pulling down after a bit a copy of *Wilt* by Tom Sharpe, a writer who sometimes makes me laugh aloud.

"Can I help you find anything?"

"Well, yes. Do you have a hymnal with music?"

"Sorry?"

"The hymnals at our church seem to have words but no music. I've been reading a biography of Thomas Hardy, which said he was greatly influenced by Isaac Watts's hymns. And I know he was a church musician with his father when he was young. So I wanted to know what the Watts hymns were and what they sound like."

Her interest in me seems to pick up. "Why, yes, I think I do." She ducks into a back room, returning with *Hymns Ancient and Modern with Tunes*. "Let's see. Here's the index. There are lots of hymns by Watts."

"Terrific." I thumb through. "Oh, sure. Here's 'Oh, God Our Help in Ages Past.' I forgot he wrote that."

"Are you doing some work on Thomas Hardy, then?"

I explain what I am doing and pull out–the schoolboy at Show and Tell—the stamps I just bought. "Here's the Hardy one."

"Oh, I know. It's been dreadful, this year. Hardy has become a huge industry here."

"I'm sure."

"My uncle knew him very well. They were friends. In fact, my uncle—an early photographer—wrote a book about the places in Hardy's books."

"No."

She shows me the book, *Thomas Hardy's Wessex*, by Hermann Lea, a collection of descriptions and black-and-white photographs of Dorset settings for the various books. I see a picture of the tower that Swithen St. Cleeves used for his astronomy in *Two on a Tower*.

"I was very fond of my uncle. He was a difficult man in some ways—reserved, suspicious. That's probably why he got on so well with Hardy, who was difficult also. But we got along very well. He always treated me like an adult. When I was ten, during the war, I stayed with him, and he took me out looking for fossils."

She pauses to close the book. "He would have been appalled by all the tourists looking around Dorset today."

I pay her for the Sharpe and the hymnal. "I may be back for your uncle's book. After all, it's part of what I'm over here for. Thank you so much."

"Nice to meet you."

My final errand in Oxford today is the insurance. The office sits right on High Street up from the bridge, newly furnished within, a long straight affair with a young male receptionist at the front and beyond a straight row of seats at a counter, behind which are perhaps ten identical young men in dark trousers, white shirts, and ties, walking to and fro or confabulating with clients. The wall behind them is shelved to the ceiling with manila folders. I suddenly realize that I am looking at the file of every policyholder in this branch of the A-Plan Insurance Company, Ltd. For all the 1990 furniture, this office probably worked the same way a century ago.

I talk with the young man who spoke to me yesterday, answering questions, filling out forms. I am not eligible for a Safe Driver's Discount. But my check is accepted, and I walk out the door, insured, assured, reassured.

Bright and early Wednesday morning I drove the car up to Young's Garage for its MOT inspection. The garage building used to be the old train station for Woodstock; the line used to run from here right along the embankment across the street from Hereford House, where the blackberries grow. The Youngs bought the station and the embankment as well when the line was discontinued in 1955. The mechanic says he'll have the car ready by four. I tell him he can do whatever repairs he must, but to call us if there's a problem. Then I stroll home, where I find the family eating breakfast.

This morning Jane is taking Sam to the morning service at St. Mary Magdalene's and then they are busing up to Chipping Norton to explore and get tickets to *Wessex Days*. This is not an adaptation of a particular Hardy story, but bits from many of them, intending I suppose to show local Wessex color. Perhaps feeling that it sounds too esoteric for her lukewarm interest in Hardy, she has decided not to go, but the Browns and I will. I have gotten her hooked on *Persuasion*, however; if we find a theater presenting a Jane Austen adaptation, she'll be there.

Having finished *Young Thomas Hardy* by Robert Gittens, I have set aside today to play with the Watts hymns and Hardy's *Wessex Poems*. At first the process is quite mechanical, making lists of poems by meter and number of stanzas, of hymns by meter alone. The latter task is a snap because the hymnal indexes them by meter as well as author, composer, tune title, and first line. Most hymns are written in one of three meters—short, which is a quatrain of two lines of iambic trimeter, one of tetrameter, and one of trimeter; common, a quatrain of alternating tetrameter and trimeter; and long, a quatrain of tetrameter. In *Wessex Poems* I find one poem of short meter, eleven of common, and five of long. In the hymnal, Watts seems to have shown similar propensities: one of short, six of common, four of long.

Longer poems won't work well in short settings, for too many repetitions of the tune flatten their development. After trying several poem/hymn pairings, I find one that makes sense. Watts's "Before Jehovah's awful throne" is a severe little homily: "Know that the Lord is God alone; / He can create, and He destroy." The tune, "Penshurst," was written four years before Hardy's birth by Vincent Novello, an organist, composer, and musical editor of the early nineteenth century. Thus Hardy may well have heard this hymn sung to this tune, a dark yet sweet march to the grave: "When rolling years shall cease to move."

The poem for which this seems apposite is "She—At His Funeral." Robert Gittens suggests that it may have been a partial response to Hardy's friend Horace Moule's suicide: a woman watches her lover's burial, the family dressed in trappings of bereavement but feeling nothing, she in her street clothes excluded from the ceremony yet consumed with grief.

As I work the tune and the words together at the piano—clumsily, for I am unskilled, untrained, purest of amateurs—I grow increasingly excited, ready next year to resurrect the Dickinsingers, get them into a rehearsal room, and hand this to the soprano, telling her the last line is a solo, to be spit out in repressed fury like acid.

They bear___ him to___ his rest - ing place, In slow___ pro-
Un - chang'd__ my gown___ of gar - ish dye; Though sa - ble

cess - ion sweep - ing by; I fol - low at___ a
sad___ is their___ at - tire; But they___ stand round___ with

stran - ger's space; His kin - dred they,__ his sweet - heart I.
grief - less eye, Whilst my___ re - gret con - sumes___ like fire.

I am still working at this task when the family returns from school.

"Guess what, Dad!" says Gardner, keeping his lips over his teeth, with effort resisting a smile.

"What?"

"I lost a tooth!" And the gap springs into view from behind his grin and his pride. He holds up a small twist of paper.

"Wow! So you did." I pretend bafflement. "Let's see. Does the Tooth Fairy operate in England?"

"Yes, she does," he replies at once. "Peter lost a tooth, and she put money under his pillow."

"Well, there. How much did she leave him?"

"I don't know."

"We'll just have to wait and see," says my wife.

He is in the best mood I've seen since school started. In the last days he has not gotten any more enthusiastic about school, nor have I heard about any new friends. Perhaps this evidence of maturity, this small rite of passage will set him back on track among his peers.

It is late the next afternoon before the Maxi is road-ready, new bushings in the suspension, current registration disk on the windshield. The whole process cost nearly £300, about the price of the car itself. "It needs some body work, I'm afraid," said the mechanic. "Some welding. You'll need to have that done for your next inspection, probably." I'm not worried about that. In a year I'll be back in the Volvo driving on the right.

The United Kingdom Tooth Fairy, Ltd., visited us last night, her gentle hands slipping 20p beneath Gardner's pillow. He has spent this afternoon scouring Woodstock for Teenage Mutant

Hero Turtle bubble gum cards, which had appeared a week earlier in the store next door, but which were sold out in three days. There are no cards left in any store in town. I have promised to look out for them in my travels, but he is currently very grumpy about their unavailability.

As the boys are eating chicken and peas in front of the television, Jane comes into the kitchen to tell me that she has been invited to attend the Annual General Meeting of the Movement for the Ordination of Women (MOW) next month in Birmingham. In addition to the business meeting, a feminist theology debate will be conducted, presumably allowing various feminist theologians to represent their full range, out to the very edge. One woman who will be there, Daphne Hampson, has asserted that Christianity is unredeemably patriarchal and sexist and should be abandoned. That should bring both the intellect and the emotion of everybody there to 6.3 on the Richter. "Perhaps," I say, "at just the right moment, when they're boiling over with sound and fury, you can get MOW to stage a march on the airport customs bureau and make them give us our fucking briefcase."

I say this with more humor than venom, for with the car in our possession, I don't feel the same pressure to get the briefcase as I did before Sunday. So much anxiety was tied up in the car. I should have called Don Barry weeks ago.

Then comes a call from the living room. "Mom. I can't eat any more. I have stomach cramps."

We normally all eat together at the kitchen table, but tonight Jane and I have decided to treat ourselves to take-out tandoori from a local Indian restaurant. I know next to nothing about Indian food except that it can be hotter than hell, so after the boys have been put to bed, she walks downtown to do the ordering. I look at the road atlas. Tomorrow I am planning to drive down to Hampshire to explore Jane Austen country.

Sitting in front of the television, we watch Inspector Morse and Sergeant Lewis cope with the disappearance of a schoolgirl in *Last Seen Wearing* and eat curried prawns and tandoori chicken. The food is wonderful, sweet, and aromatic. We sip wine.

"How were the boys today?" I ask.

"I'm still getting complaints about those Turtle cards. And he cried again at school and had cramps. You heard him at dinner."

"Do you think he's really sick?"

"I don't know."

At a grocery checkout counter the clerk tells Morse the cost of his purchases. Morse tells Lewis that he forged a letter from the missing girl.

"What?" says Lewis in disbelief.

"Fourteen pounds twenty-eight," says the clerk.

We have seen this episode before, and laugh.

Later, as we are preparing to go upstairs, we hear a wail, then loud sobbing.

"It's Gardner," says Jane, dashing up the stairs. When I arrive, she is carrying him into our room. "It's all right," she is saying. "We'll fix it. You lie on our bed." When she comes back out in the hall, she says quietly, "He wet his bed."

"Oh, God." He hasn't wet the bed since he was two. Together we strip the bed and change the linen.

When he is back in his own bed, we sit beside him. "How do you feel now?" I ask.

"My stomach aches."

"Well, try to get to sleep."

"I can't." In a faint keening, sounding like a grieving widow in the next room, he moans, rolling away from us, knees drawn up in a fetal position.

We each stoop over to kiss his cheek. "Well, try."

Still later, as we lie in bed in the dark, we hear his door open and his feet move to the bathroom. Then the toilet flushes and he pushes open our door. "Mommy. Dad. I threw up, but it's O.K. I did it in the toilet." He sounds composed, controlled, the Rational Philosopher.

As Jane gets up to help him back to bed, I think to myself, "Jesus Christ. Something is wrong. Something is really wrong."

9

I am driving down the A34 toward Hampshire, the morning having broken clear and bright. It's a straight shot south. I pass on the east the power station at Didcot, conventional energy I'm told, not nuclear, which we saw looking west from the train to London. In light of Gardner's illness I considered not going at all today, but at breakfast Jane pressed me. "He seems O.K. right now. I'm going to send him to school. It will be good practice for your driving. Then tomorrow we can all go up to Warwick, so the boys can see the castle."

"If he's up to it."

The sun pours through the mist hanging over the fields of mown hay, and I think of Keats's "season of mists and mellow fruitfulness." Though I love this poem, I don't have it memorized; still, a couple of lines—"close bosom-friend of the maturing sun"; "thy hair soft-lifted by the winnowing wind"—return, caressing me, soothing my conscience. After I get off the A34 near Kingsclere, I pull over to photograph a Keatsian autumn field, cows grazing in the mist, great sprays of willow-herb (fireweed in America) growing pinkly at the pasture gate.

Jane Austen was born in 1775 in Steventon, a tiny village about fifteen miles north of Winchester, where her father was rector of the village parish. Unlike Mr. Collins, the pompous clergyman in *Pride and Prejudice,* he was witty and wise; and unlike Mr. Bennet in the same book, he had six sons and only two daughters—which meant he did not have to worry about his daughters after he died, for even if they did not marry—which they did not—their brothers could support them—which they did.

I have trouble finding Steventon and turn finally in desperation onto what a sign tells me is a "single-track road." It is a harrowing passage, winding narrowly between high hedgerows. Another car confronts me and I must back up to let it pass. A woman walking her dogs helps me; I am in Ibworth, she tells me, four miles north of the road I should be on. At last I find Deane, the Austens' neighboring village. A double-track road from Deane passes through a tunnel beneath a huge railway embankment. When I emerge on the other side, there is the village center: three roads intersecting at a sort of town hall. There is no store, no post office, no petrol station. I park in front of the town hall.

Several houses are gathered about, skirted by fields of green and cows. A train hoots along the track above the village. Although the old Austen rectory has long been destroyed, I understand that an old pump is supposed to stand at the site. I look in the various fields but can see no such article. An elderly bearded gentleman is doing some early morning gardening in front of one of the houses, so I approach him.

"Oh, yes," he says. "The pump was just beyond the hall there. But it's been taken away, I'm afraid. Souvenir hunters." He shakes his head, and the beard quivers regretfully. "But come inside. We have a painting of it."

In his living room hangs a small oil, no masterpiece but clear enough, of a rusted pump surrounded by a metal fence, beyond which lies a field and farther a house. "That house is the 'new' rectory, built by Jane Austen's brother when he inherited the position from his father. You can see it down the road. An American bought it and is restoring it." He pauses. "The pump's fence is still there."

His middle-aged daughter has come into the room behind us. "Now, go see the church," she says. "And come back in the spring when the snowdrops are in bloom. Jane Austen wrote about them in her letters, and they are a lovely sight."

I follow signs up a tree-lined drive to the church: St. Nicholas's, small, gray stone, well-kept, exquisite. Inside in a rear corner, for a few pence each, Jane Austen postcards and pamphlets are offered for sale. Memorial plaques for her father, mother, and brother James (who succeeded his father as rector in Steventon) are set near the altar on the wall of the sanctuary. Outside, gravestones cant mossily in the tiny churchyard. A great tree shades the front. I set up my tripod and photograph inside and out. The only sound is the occasional click of the camera; otherwise I am awash in silence and warm sun.

The Austens lived in Steventon for the first twenty-six years of Jane's life. During that time she wrote versions of *Pride and Prejudice* (originally called *First Impressions*), *Sense and Sensibility*, and *Northanger Abbey*. She spent most of her last eight years in Chawton, perhaps ten miles away. In between she lived unhappily in Bath until her father died and then in Southampton with one of her brothers. She hated being away from the country. Although she tried to write a novel while in Bath—*The Watsons*—she abandoned it after her father's death in 1805. Returning to Hampshire in 1809 to a house owned by Edward Knight, the richest of her brothers, she wrote her last three novels—*Mansfield Park, Persuasion,* and *Emma*—and began another, *Sanditon,* which was interrupted by her death.

Chawton seems a much more substantial village than Steventon, and the Jane Austen House a more substantial part of the local economy than a missing pump. A number of tourists are gathering at the gate when I arrive, just before the ten o'clock opening, all of us respectful, hushed. The garden is carefully tended, bright with flowers even in autumn. I walk around the house with the camera, finally settling on a bench in the sunshine.

A woman in a bright cotton dress arrives, and a pound gains me admittance to the house. In the front room are display cases of Austen memorabilia, including jewelry, letters, music, and a lock of her hair, which is light brown. In the next room a bookcase holds many first editions and foreign language translations. In the Cyrillic alphabet *EMMA* is at once recognizable, but *Mansfield Park* begins to retreat into obscurity: *МАНСФЕИЛД ПАРК.*

A door leading to the stairs is marked "The Creaking Door." She would never allow its hinges to be oiled, because its squeak warned her of visitors, giving her a chance to put away her writing. The Chawton house is wonderfully preserved and maintained, but—unlike Steventon, which seems still somehow alive with her presence—Jane has clearly departed this place. Ghosts seldom hang about museums.

Suffering from Addison's Disease in 1817, she went to Winchester for treatment during the last two months of her life; so I follow her there. The house she stayed in is not far from Winchester Cathedral, a simple yellow wooden building bearing a plaque commemorating her days there.

Upon entering the cathedral, I pay a pound fee to take photographs, but for a while only wander about. She is buried in the north aisle. On the wall just above her gravestone is a brass plaque, erected by two of her brothers to announce that the anonymous "lady" who had written *Sense and Sensibility* and those other wonderful novels (for the author was during her life-time designated "A Lady") was in fact their beloved sister Jane. Many more tourists than were present at Chawton are here, gazing reverently upward at the great vaulted ceiling and then down at the long black stone that marks her grave. A number of art students are scattered about, drawing capitals and columns in charcoal. In a small side chapel is the grave of Izaac Walton, the great fisherman, whose presence there is celebrated by a pair of stained-glass windows of reels and creels, trout, and several compleat anglers.

After a time I sit in the north aisle and photograph the sun-light glinting against the polished brass plaque beside her grave. Before it stands a vase of yellow and orange chrysanthemums. Suddenly, perhaps set in motion by those autumnal colors, "To Autumn" is echoing again in my brain.

I have a book, *Blue Guide to Literary Britain and Ireland,* which arranges travel information not by place, but by author. Sitting in a pew near her grave, I read of Steventon, of her time in Bath, of her return to Chawton:

> Our Chawton Home, how much we find
> > Already in it to our mind;
> And how convinced, that when complete
> > It will all other houses beat
> That ever have been made or mended,
> > With rooms concise or rooms distended.

On a whim I turn to Keats's pages: "From the Isle of Wight, he moved north to Winchester, where he spent the autumn months of 1819 just before his final departure from England and where he wrote his 'Ode to Autumn.'"

Before today, the juxtaposition of Jane Austen, Miss Sense, and John Keats, Mr. Sensibility, would never have occurred to me, never; and yet here they are, Keats describing Winchester as "the pleasantest Town I ever was in," the Cathedral as "fine," and doing so only two years after Jane Austen was buried in this very spot. All at once the whole word-woven tapestry becomes finer, tighter. This is why I have come here, to learn this: English literature was not a collection of pigeonholes of Augustan and Romantic and Victorian and Bloomsbury to those who were writing it. It was—and still is—indivisible and organic, woven into whole cloth from the retold experience of men and women who lived together on this small green island. A kind of joy fills me, stays with me all the way back to Woodstock, as over my head the gathering swallows twitter in the skies.

When I return, it is about five o'clock. Gardner does not look away from *Duck Tales* as I come in. Jane's face is grim. I realize with a flash of guilt that I have not wondered about them all day.

"How did it go?"

"O.K.," she says. "But I have a doctor's appointment for him on Monday at the surgery."

"Was he sick again today?"

"No. But since he got home from school, he's been a total pain."

"Tomorrow. Do we want to go to Warwick Castle?"

"Hey," he says, coming into the kitchen. "When do we eat? I'm hungry."

"If we can. He wants to go."

"No kidding," I say to him. "That's nice to hear."

"Soon," says Jane. "I'm cooking northern Italian noodles."

"Yuck. I want ravioli."

"This has been going on for an hour," she says to me.

"But you like northern Italian noodles. We have it at home all the time."

"I want ravioli." He is beyond Le Misérable in an instant, fully The Whiner. We are one refusal away from The Basket Case.

"You can try the noodles," says my wife in a tight voice.

"I never get anything I want," wails The Basket Case.

"All right, damn it."

Instantly the sun returns to his eyes. "Thank you, Mommy." He is now The Cutest Child in the World.

Desperate to find something that will break through his growing finickiness, all this week Jane has been looking for American-style food. She turned up a can of ravioli in the Coop, not Chef Boyardee, but it says "ravioli" on the label. He didn't rise to its appeal when she brought it home, but this evening he is scrabbling after it with manic desire, at the same time obviously driving his mother closer and closer to the wall.

We are all at the table, Sam in his high chair noodling with sautéed egg and spaghetti, as Jane and I hold our breaths and watch a piece of ravioli rise to the mouth, enter, and disappear. *Splat!* He spits it back on his plate. Tears fill his eyes. "I don't like it. It doesn't taste good."

Jane's eyebrows crash over her eyes, and her mouth grows thin and straight as a razor. She stands up. "I could slug him," she says to me in a low voice.

Understand, Jane does not talk this way ever. Except for football she detests all physical violence—from what is happening now in the Persian Gulf down to a swat on an errant bottom.

All the five and a half years we've known this boy she has never spanked him or countenanced my doing so. The only time she ever used force with him was to slap his hands when he would not stop playing with electrical plugs and sockets. It is as if someone else is here, and my heart freezes.

"Hey," I say.

But she walks out of the kitchen. "You deal with him. I can't."

That night she weeps, bitterly, fearfully; and later—into the casserole dish I set by his bed—he vomits once again.

10

As one walks or drives about Warwick, the castle towers loom suddenly over a row of trees or buildings like giants surprised. It would be possible to ramble around for quite a while, to shop or eat, and not to realize the castle's presence. A wall separates it from the town; set on a bluff over the Avon with the business district behind and slightly above, it is fully defensible from a river attack but seems vulnerable at the rear, to an uprising of citizens, some sort of Peasants' (or Burghers') Revolt. Indeed, this happens now nearly every day as rapacious tourists like us fall upon it with our cameras and our curiosity.

I notice the castle's unobtrusiveness at once, for I'm not clear where we should park the car, despite small signs for "Castle Parking." I know that once I commit myself to a route there will be no turning back; if we find ourselves in a car park with a £10 price tag, we'll eat that instead of lunch. I'm edgy enough because of my sick son. We decided to come even though he has held virtually nothing in his stomach for a week. He is pale, thin, irritable, lethargic. I have visions of him collapsing in tears, of all of us inside with the fees paid being forced to leave immediately to drive fifty miles back home, sadder and not a whit wiser. So I whip the car around the town once or twice, occasionally surprised by a tower leaping out from behind a tree, until finally I say to myself, "What the hell," and turn us into the ground's car park lane.

Hereford House came equipped with a stroller, luckily since we could not bring ours with us among the welter of equipment on the plane. This one is blue with small double front wheels, battered and bent but unbowed by our friends' two children—and others, perhaps—as they were strolled about Woodstock, Blenheim, Oxford, and beyond. We have not brought it along to Warwick for Sam, not a hope; as we move up the lane from the car park, Sam rides jauntily on my shoulders and beside us my wife pushes Gardner, who is folded into the stroller, his knees hanging over the padded restraining bar.

We are not uncheerful as we walk. "Look at that tower," I say. There is no comment, but I sense a faint scent of enthusiasm rising from the stroller. At the entrance I pay £13.50—around $25, as we are figuring the pound—and we walk and roll across the bridge over the dry grassy moat and through a gateway in the wall. The walkways have turned to gravel.

"You'll have to walk now," says Jane.

"Why?"

"Hey," I say, spotting a sign. "Look, over there. The torture chamber and the dungeons."

His ears prick up. "What?"

"The dungeons. You know what they are. Come on."

He jerks out of the stroller onto his feet. The bounce has left his step, but he's balanced firmly enough to suggest some energy, a quick shot of adrenaline probably. He certainly can't be running on what's in his stomach. He ate half a roll this morning, which except for some apple juice is the only thing he's held down since yesterday noon when he confronted whatever his school lunch was. It is hard to imagine where last night he found anything to vomit.

The stairway to the dungeon is so narrow that two adults can barely pass side-to-side, let alone shoulder-to-shoulder. A group is emerging, but it doesn't slow him a bit. He burrows through their legs like a ferret, lithe and slim and quick.

"Wait," I call, but it's too late. Finally the rest of us get an open passage down the stone stairs, into which are worn two- or three-inch depressions by the tread of centuries of stern gaolers and broken traitors. We arrive into a room that contains several instruments of torture on display: iron masks, thumbscrews, a rack, some sort of body cage hanging above our heads.

He is standing in the middle, his mouth slightly open.

"Look at that stuff," I tell him.

"What is it?"

Soft-pedaling the gore, I explain the functions of some of these items as I understand them, doubtless imperfectly, but he is uncritical. Cartoons and movies, Hero Turtles and He-Man, the stories of King Arthur and St. George, all of these however gracefully told touch his primordial interest in cruelty. In watching my son develop, perhaps more than in any other experience, I have sensed the underlying primitive nature of human beings, believing that one of the most profound elements of our psychological constitution is a fear of and simultaneous attraction to the infliction of pain. He looks at the apparatus with respect: real torture, concrete torture, torture one can see, worthy of He-Man's nemesis Skeletor or of Shredder, arch-enemy of the Turtles. Then we peer through the bars down into the stone pits of exitless cells. It is a vision of hell, tenantless now and disused, but surely once an infernal place. At last, thank God, I see his eyes tighten, his arms clutch to his side, faint signs of nerves. "Dad, I want to go upstairs."

We emerge into the great grassy courtyard, surrounded by the walls of the castle, where we consult the map. At our backs are Caesar's Tower, the Gateway, and Guy's Tower; to our left the palace with the State Rooms, the Great Hall, and the Private Apartments. Warwick has had earls since the twelfth century, who built these towers in the fourteenth century and this palace sometime during the reign of the Stuarts. I know the family slightly from Shakespeare. One Earl of Warwick had a bit part in *Henry V;* another gets a mention in *Richard III:* "my great father-in-law, renowned Warwick," says the Duke of Clarence just before the evil Richard has him put to death in the Tower of London.

"What do you think, buddy?" I ask. A sign for a walk along the top of the walls and up the towers warns away the faint of body or spirit: WARNING—200 STEPS.

"I want to go up on the walls."

"Are you sure you're up for it?" asks Jane. "There are two hundred steps you have to climb. That's what that sign says."

"Sure."

She goes with him while I contend with Sam. After a time we get into a line entering the palace tour, he riding my shoulders. Madame Tussaud's has provided wax figures to people the apartments, depicting a particular house party of June, 1898, with the then–Earl of Warwick and his wife, the Prince of Wales (later Edward VII), butlers, an opera singer, even the Duke and Duchess of Marlborough—up from Blenheim for a weekend of music and card playing. We are herded along single file through the rooms, until my rider begins to twist and writhe in a concerted effort to dismount. Visions fill my eyes, Sam racing under the restraining

97

cord to jump into Lady Warwick's lap, knocking the letter from her wax hand, the wig from her wax head. I clutch his legs. He squeals. It is impossible to beat our way out of here against the line of people behind us.

Craning my head about frantically, I see at last a live woman in an official-looking smock. "Excuse me. My young friend here is getting very restless. Is there a quick way out?"

She smiles. "Of course. Follow me." Quickly, magically, we are outside.

I set him on the grass, across which a peacock is strutting. Along the top of the walls I see figures, tiny in the distance. One of them, barely recognizable, waves to us. "Look. There's Mommy."

He gazes inscrutably at the end of my pointing finger, then back at the peacock. "Birt. Ooo."

When they rejoin us, Gardner's eyes are sparkling. "It was cool, Dad." His words get caught up in almost a stutter. "We were up in the, the tower, and I beat Mom."

I have no idea what he's talking about, but it makes no difference. I look at Jane. She nods, smiles happily. "He walked the whole thing. It was very cool."

During lunch thick dark clouds begin to roll across the sky. Sam, heedless of his own footing, tries to chase peacocks and ducks into the river. Predictably, after the thrill of walking the wall, things begin to unravel for Gardner. The armory was satisfactory as long as he rode on my shoulders, but the gift shop had for sale no small knights, ever since the Tower of London the only acceptable souvenir from a castle. Here in the picnic area, the food stand offers nothing that appeals. He declared the soup yucky and two sips of hot chocolate have left him feeling sick. The gravel paths are impassable by stroller. The toilet is too far to walk, way across to the formal garden of topiaries and behind the conservatory, yet we must get there. Hymns of sorrow, hymns of sadness, whines and whimpers now are raised; charge these boys with grateful gladness, through them let these days be praised. To the tune of "Stuttgart." Amen.

"I don't want to ride over to church," he sobs. "I want Inspector Gadget." It's Sunday morning, the glories of Warwick departed after a night of crying and finally vomiting into the casserole dish beside his bed. After he got up this morning, he did not want to get dressed, nor eat breakfast, and now he doesn't want to leave his cartoons.

Jane is thrumming like a fiddle string. "Look," she says. "I'll put it on the VCR. You can see it when you get back. You won't miss a thing."

"I don't want to."

"I can't drive myself, and we can't leave you alone."

"I don't care. I won't go."

I feel like strangling him, but before I can say anything, she explodes. "Damn you, Gardner. You are so selfish. You are a self-centered brat." She bursts into angry tears and storms into the kitchen.

"All right," I say, dropping into my bass registers for authority. "We're all going. There won't be any more damn cartoons at all."

"Noooo!" he wails.

I turn off the set. "O.K., Jane. We're going."

"Noooo, Daddy!" he weeps and kicks on the couch. "I won't go!"

Sam's eyes are large; he waddles toward the kitchen to offer comfort, to make peace. "Mommy."

She, however, is back at the door. "That's all right. The selfish baby can stay. I won't go."

She is furious, in physical control maybe but throwing words

99

at him like knives. It is hard to say whether they are having any effect, so completely is he consumed in the flames of his own passion. Sam and I are like Shadrach and Meshach caught between two fiery furnaces.

"Wrong," I say. "We are all going to take Mom to church. And we are leaving right now."

"I won't!"

I pick him up flailing and weeping, toss him over my shoulder like a sack of angry chickens. Out the door and through the gate and across the street he is carried, borne on the cresting wave of my own clean fine emotion to the cargo area of the Maxi, where he is dumped and the door is slammed. Behind me, already bearing the weight of gathering guilt and shame and remorse, comes Jane, who carries Sam in her arms also.

We take the back road to Wootton, a route I rode on my bicycle a couple weeks ago one afternoon. Soon the sobbing in the back of the car quiets, and by the time we reach the church—not more than ten minutes—all passion is spent.

"What will you do?"

"Drive around a bit. Maybe look for some place we can go for lunch. We'll be back in an hour and a half."

"Thanks."

I watch her walk through the stone gate toward the church. What will her prayers be like today? I wonder. Some for forgiveness, surely, even though she shouldn't need it. I saw her guilt at getting angry at him, but who wouldn't get angry at such intractability? She'll pray for strength, too, I hope. And deliverance. From things that go bump in the night, good Lord, deliver us, goes the old Scottish prayer. For understanding and deliverance? But we can't always accept what happens, nor should we, it seems to me; when things get too horrible, acceptance turns grotesque. I knew a man once, a Christian Scientist, whose daughter died of stomach cancer before his eyes. His acceptance, his stolidity, his failure to rail and shake his fists against the dreadful demands of the Almighty, seemed to me inhuman. Abraham on the mountain, Isaac across the altar, the sacrificial knife high in the air: where are the limits of faith?

Make him well, loving God.

An even greater set of questions has to do with what is actually happening to my son. Lying quiescent in the back of the Maxi sucking his thumb, he reflects—on what? Does he remember his anger this morning? Does he regret it? Where does the source of this pain lie, and how may we root it out, pull it from him like an infected tooth and restore the productive, handsome little boy we have had for five years? Although he can talk, often precisely about events that please or interest him, we should not be fooled into believing he can articulate—even to himself—the sources of his sorrow. He is only five. His prayers can only exist in the concrete—give me Teenage Mutant Hero Turtle cards or a morning of cartoons instead of church or the Woodstock Primary School. He asks for deliverance, wanting nothing to do with understanding, nor acceptance, nor forgiveness, nor even strength—at least explicitly.

When we pick up my wife after church, she looks happier, restored. "It was a good service. I saw Alistair Wallworth." This last to Gardner: Alistair is a schoolmate of his, and a nice boy to boot.

"Good. We drove around for a while, then went home. Things went fine."

"Great. Where are we going for lunch?"

In fact we saw no restaurant nor pub that interested the boys in Wootton nor Bladon nor any of the other places we explored. Suddenly I have it, Eureka, and I'm running naked through the streets. "Let's go to McDonald's!"

"Yay!" says Gardner. "McDonald's!"

Off we go to Oxford, where on Cornmarket Street we find not only the McDonald's but also Burger King, which with certain meals is giving away a pair of MicroMachines, tiny cars and trucks Gardner much admires. So into BK we go, where he eats almost an entire cheeseburger with ketchup, and a few french fries. Jane and I are filled with thanksgiving and joy.

In the afternoon I drive alone to Begbroke, where a neighbor of ours, Joe Freeman, is playing for the town's cricket team. By now I have a reasonably good understanding of the game. A team of eleven men bats until all but one are out; then the other team takes its turn. The field is elliptical, with a set of wickets—three sticks in the ground with two small pieces of wood balanced on top of them—about twenty yards apart at each of the two foci of the ellipse. A bowler takes a running start and hurls the ball straight-arm over his head toward one wicket, which is defended by a batsman. Another batsman waits at the other wicket. If the bowler knocks over the wicket, the batsman will be out, so he hits the ball, either blocking it away or swinging for distance. On long hits the batsman races to change ends, thus scoring runs. If a ball rolls beyond the perimeter of the ellipse, four runs are awarded; if it flies beyond, six. If the ball is caught in the air, or the wicket broken before the batsman reaches it, an out is recorded.

It is hard to get batsmen out. No field players wear gloves except one, the wicket keeper, who handles the bowled balls like a baseball catcher. The ball, as hard as a baseball, can be bowled with frightening velocity, and it can rocket off the bat even faster. There are long periods of inactivity followed by an instant of explosive activity, making concentration for the fielders difficult.

Test matches, played by the national teams, last for three days. In order to finish a town game in an afternoon, the number of overs each side bats is limited, often to forty. An over is a unit of six balls bowled at one wicket, after which a different bowler must come in from the field and bowl to the other. A shutout over is called a "maiden." A bowler who has allowed no runs in his six bowls has "bowled a maiden over."

When I arrive, the match is in progress, two women on lawn chairs watching the activity from near the gate. The rest of the batting team is lounging in front of the clubhouse. "Which team is which?" I ask the women.

"Begbroke is in the field," one replies.

"Oh, good. My neighbor plays, and I came to see him."

"Who's that?"

"Joe Freeman."

"Oh, Joe. He's quite a good player, really. There he is, across the field."

It's a great distance, and, scattered about the field in their white shirts and slacks, all the men look alike. At last from a group of three I make him out. A heavy young man, standing in the batter's crease closest to us, blocks a ball down into the dirt.

"How are we doing?" *We:* already I am a hometown fan.

"Two are out. Probably about twenty-five or thirty runs by now, I expect."

I look around, but there is no scoreboard. Back on the field, the heavy young batsman takes a terrific cut and the ball peels in a high arc over the fence, banging the roof of a house. "Wow."

Cheering erupts from the group of players in front of the clubhouse.

"Six more in any case," says one of the women.

The afternoon wears on, the sun slanting across the field. In another over, the heavy young batsman is dismissed, caught out on a short fly ball by the wicket keeper. Later I watch Joe bowl two or three overs. The players break for tea. I chat with the scorers and inspect their massive scorebooks. Begbroke comes to bat. I drift around the edges of the game, remembering town baseball games back in the States, warm sun and grass, cries of laughter and exaltation and triumph. Then, the players still celebrating the game's timeless liturgy, I return to Hereford House and my fragile son.

11

*L*isa is sitting in the car beside me, rattling away in the rich accents of home, washing my soul with hope. She is a Californian from Cupertino, a massage therapist working for a Woodstock chiropractor, married to a USAF technician stationed at the base near Lower Heyford. Their son, Jordan, who is almost two, is back at Hereford House playing with Jane and Sam.

This week so far has been dreadful, unimaginably so. Gardner has vomited five times in the last three days. Mornings he has been left at school weeping violently and clutching at Jane. We are both afraid the other kids will turn away from him even if he ever does start to settle down. After school he is listless or whiny. At meals he eats very little and then vomits. Last night he refused spaghetti, then peanut butter and jam. Not jelly. Jelly here is a brick which, dissolved in boiling water, turns into Jell-O. In fact Jane recently made some jelly/Jell-O, to offer to him as a last resort; he accepted three bites, which reappeared almost immediately.

On Monday he did not go to school, and in the afternoon Jane took him to the surgery. They saw Dr. Swift, who could find nothing wrong with him and simply tried to reassure her. "He said he's never heard of a five-year-old developing a serious eating disorder," she reported. "He says it will pass. We should just give him what he wants."

"Great. They're sold out of Turtle cards. The hot dogs here are made of boiled suet. How the hell are we going to give him what he wants?"

"I know, I know," she said gently. Somehow as this week has darkened, the fury inside her has dissipated. She seems calmer, quieter, though sadder.

And I am winding myself tighter. I agree with Dr. Swift. I cannot believe that he has an organic disturbance; I think if we can only give him what he wants, we can get him back to the table. What is an eating disorder, anyway? I never had one, God knows, except maybe in wanting to eat too much. At eight I moved from a Boston suburb to Portland, Maine, with anticipation and excitement. My younger sister was different, though. She hated change, especially if it was geographic. When my parents sent her away for two weeks of summer camp, she raised such a fuss they had to bring her home after five days. What will Gardner require? Can we ever make England a dish he will consume?

Surprisingly in the middle of all this stress, we have actually had some social activity. On Sunday, after I returned from the cricket match, we put the boys to bed and went to dinner at the Browns'. We found a baby-sitter, who arrived at quarter to eight to read *Stuart Little* to Gardner, and walked across the street. The Browns invited another couple as well, themselves parents of two young children. The conversations ranged through teaching and in-laws and Thomas Hardy and photography, returning now and again to the themes of health and children, a not unpleasant but nevertheless sober evening. Now, three days later, I can remember little that was actually said, only a sensation that the other couple was also under some sort of stress, for reasons that seemed to do more with marital dynamics than with progeny. Still, when we got home, we decided we were pleased with ourselves for getting out on our own, for creating two and a half hours of freedom together.

Then last night the Browns and I, Martyn driving, went up to Chipping Norton to "The Theater," to see *Wessex Days,* by Sean Street. In a small intimate space four actors—two men, two women—fairly filled the bare stage as they presented a gallery of Hardy's people, mostly members of the folk chorus that makes his work so rich: the Durbeyfields, the Dewys from *Under the Greenwood Tree,* Amos Fry from *Two on a Tower,* and lots of others whom I will meet as I read more novels. As there wasn't a story line to speak of and as some of the scenes were a bit more local than colorful, it was probably just as well that Jane gave this the miss. I found myself reacting more like a teacher than a theatergoer, looking for routines I might use in the classroom.

Last year I taught to a class of tenth-graders a Hardy poem, "The Ruined Maid"—a dramatic dialogue between a farm girl and her friend who has gone to the big city and is now having a wonderful time as a "ruined" woman, with good food and flashy clothes. The two actresses hammed this up with abandon, but then segued into the pathetic speech of Tess Durbeyfield, who, having returned home pregnant and unmarried, berates her mother for not warning her about the tragedy of being seduced. "I was a child when I left this house. Why didn't you tell me there was danger in menfolk, Mother? Why didn't you warn me?"

"I thought if I spoke of his fond feelings and what they might lead to, you would be hontish with him and lose your chance. I just wanted the best for you, Tessie," came the pitiful response, the guilt-stricken voice of all parents. "The best": what else do we want for our children?

I'm not sure when we heard about Lisa. It may have been at the dinner on Sunday. Whenever, it was Jane Brown, hearing our difficulty in interesting Gardner in food, who said, "Look. You should talk with Lisa. Her husband works at the Air Force base, and she might be able to get you some American food there."

So now I'm driving north, ten miles from Woodstock, begging for help from the United States Air Force. "It's such a shame," says Lisa. "Poor little guy."

"It's very nice of you to do this."

"No, I'm glad for the ride. I usually don't get to get away. My husband has the car most of the time."

She is pregnant and heavy, a sturdy woman with the appearance of mass rather than fat, with a round cheerful face and powerful arms. Jane Brown—who is interested in all forms of medicine, traditional and holistic alike—spoke of receiving a massage at her hands: "Golly! She pushed me right round. I didn't know if I would live through it, you know, but afterwards I felt quite peachy." Looking at her arms, I imagine she could crack the most stubborn of adhesions. I think of the way Gardner hunches when the cramps knot his neck and back and calves. Maybe chiropractic can help.

Lord knows, I'm desperate enough for anything. Last night I tried to hypnotize him.

When I was in junior high school, a hypnotist from I think Arizona wrote a book called *The Search for Bridy Murphy*, describing a subject, a housewife who under hypnosis recalled a previous life as an Irishwoman named Bridy Murphy. Like many others I was fascinated, not so much with the elements of reincarnation as with hypnotism itself. Later in high school a friend demonstrated the process at a party, and I tried it on others, even on myself, with varying degrees of success.

Always I have had a great respect for the human psyche, and I felt very leery of doing damage once I cracked into someone's skull. I read whatever I could find, looking out for pitfalls so as to avoid them, giving my subjects short-term and banal post-hypnotic suggestions, such as taking off a shoe or scratching an armpit when hearing the word "Chicago." I had no desire to push anyone under the whirring blades of psychosis.

Despite what Dr. Swift said, I am firmly convinced that it is tension and stress causing Gardner to weep and cramp and vomit. So last night, with the three bites of jelly/Jell-O returned to the casserole dish and the prospect of cramps and weeping fits during the night, I asked him if he wanted to try a special relaxing technique.

"O.K." He sounded dubious.

As I had done thirty years ago with my high school friends, I took a coin from my pocket and set it before him. He sat at the small table in his room. "I want you to put your arms on the table and look at this penny. See how big and round it is. Pretend now that your arms are heavy, heavy. Pretend that they are full of lead, and feel how heavy they are. Just relax and feel heavy."

Once under hypnosis he could be soothed, his muscles loosened, his stomach unknotted. Perhaps I could even make him look kindly upon the school, upon the food, upon the new country. One step at a time, though: for now I would try to give him a good night's sleep.

I worked to make my voice monotonous and calm, which was a lie because I felt nervous, frightened even, because I was growing fearful that somewhere within him there lies something, great pain or sorrow or anguish or anger, from a source I fear I cannot begin to understand, and if my hypnotizing him were to unleash it, God knows what would happen, how to bring it under control, it would be like trying to cap a gusher or a geyser. Please let me say the right thing, I was thinking.

He heard my fear through my voice, I am sure, for he stopped me. "I don't want to do this, Daddy," he said, and with relief I gave it up.

"We met in Texas," Lisa is saying. "We were going to the same church." We are driving across a sort of rising plain, wide-fenced empty fields beneath a gray sky. "Turn right up here," she says.

Suddenly buildings loom up on the right; on the left is a high berm, beyond which I feel sure are runways. She points to one of the buildings. "That's the bowling alley. And over there is the doughnut shop. Maybe he'd like some doughnuts."

Doughnuts! I love doughnuts, and the very word fills me with nostalgia. I nearly weep with the desire to be sitting at the pink Formica counter back home, dunking a Dunkin Donut into a cup of coffee, my son sleek and happy at the day-care center, all of this having never happened. But I say only, "A great idea."

"Turn left here."

Suddenly in front of me is a red octagonal sign: STOP. "Look!" I cry. "A stop sign!" I have not seen one since August 12.

"Yeah," says Lisa happily.

"Do we drive on the right on the base?" I am serious. Is this a little island of America surrounded by the mighty ocean of Britannia? Are all the laws of England suspended here, the way in Gardner's *Sky Turtles* cartoon an antigravity device negates the law of gravity? If we bring him here, set him here for an hour, will he be magically set right to eat doughnuts and butterscotch pudding and Hostess Twinkies?

"No," says Lisa.

I park beside the commissary, a gray windowless warehouse

of a building. As a civilian I cannot go inside, so I give Lisa a pair of twenty dollar bills—half our stash of U.S. currency—and our list of Kraft Macaroni and Cheese Dinner, Oscar Mayer Wieners, Cap'n Crunch, Froot Loops, Wonder Bread, Royal Butterscotch Pudding, Skippy Peanut Butter, Bisquick, Spaghetti-O's, Rice-a-Roni: much that Jane and I left behind with pleasure and that our son pines for today. It's food with no lumps, homogenized, whipped, and blended. I remember the old radio jingle: "Royal Pudding, rich-rich-rich in flavor, smooth-smooth-smooth like silk, more food energy than good fresh milk."

After twenty minutes or so Lisa returns, carrying two paper bags of groceries. "I got most of it. I also tried some other stuff. Let's see." She pokes into one of the sacks. "Brownie mix. He'll like that, won't he?" I nod. "And Kool-Aid. All kids like that. And some pork and beans. And here's some Chef Boyardee ravioli."

He'll never touch pork and beans, and ravioli is off the list now, but what the hell, this outlay is wonderful in every other respect. Some of it has to break through his defenses and land in his stomach. I'm talking to myself as if his self-starvation has been deliberate, that he is a small Dick Gregory or Mahatma Gandhi making a point, but this isn't so. He is, I am certain, out of control, but surely not irrevocably so. With the packages of bait in the backseat, we can lure him back.

Lisa and I stop at the doughnut shop, where I treat us each to a doughnut and coffee and buy half a dozen to take home. I also buy a paper, *Stars and Stripes,* where I read that, although pitcher Roger Clemens's shoulder is healthy again, the Boston Red Sox have fallen into a tie for first place with the Toronto Blue Jays in the Eastern Division of the American League, which they had led for over a month. There used to be a joke in Boston that the Sox would be sold and moved to the Philippines, where they would be renamed the Manila Folders.

Stars and Stripes seems relaxed about what's happening in the Persian Gulf, just another day at the office. A month ago President Bush called up 40,000 reservists; last week the Iraqis were roughing up foreign diplomats in Kuwait City. Saddam Hussein has recently appeared on television ruffling the hair of a British child hostage. This display of avuncular affection for juvenile "human shields" has thoroughly roiled the British press, for as in America children in trouble can set a nation quivering. A couple years ago in Texas it was Baby Jessica stuck down a well; when we first arrived here, the papers were full of a little girl named Gemma who had disappeared from her home, kidnapped as it turned out by a dysfunctional neighbor. I wonder what the press would make of Gardner, who seems to be a sort of hostage in a strange country. *Stars and Stripes* has little to say about child hostages, today anyhow. Still, it looks like war is coming, and I'm not sure how I feel as I read the profiles of American men and women calmly eager, even calmly joyful, "to do the job we've been sent here to do."

On the way home I ask Lisa, "Do you ever work on children?"

"Once in a while. Not very often. But I sure could."

"I don't know. His muscles get so tight. Maybe a massage would help." As I think about him, though, it won't work. He hates to be touched by strangers, and he can be so uncooperative with doctors that I doubt she can work with him.

"Poor little guy," she says again, and I let it drop.

After lunch I ride my bicycle down to Mr. Taylor's electrical shop. The transformer for the computer arrived a week ago, but a set of different plugs were necessary to pump the altered current into the machines. Three components require power: the printer, the monitor, and the computer itself. Mr. Taylor called while Lisa and I were shopping to report that at last he has the answer.

It turns out to be an extension box for four three-pronged fused plugs, which are neither standard American nor standard British design. He has wired this device to the transformer, which is the only element with a British plug. "That way nobody will stick anything in where it doesn't belong," he explains. He shows me which wire to attach to which screw inside the plug—the "live," the "neutral," and the "earth," which in America we call the "ground." The entire assembly costs nearly £50. Full of hope for some sort of solid accomplishment, I pedal it home.

The attachment of the new plugs is not difficult, but when I turn on the power, something is wrong. The printer responds to its test command, the monitor lights up with the Apple logo, but the disk drive just spins around. I try several programs, but nothing will load. It's an old drive, nine or ten years old, whose partner died two years ago. I go downstairs.

"How's it working?" All the familiar food has made her optimistic.

I try to sound as if I know what I'm saying. "The disk drive is dead. I think."

"Oh no."

My first thought is to check with dealers here. I have seen advertisements for Apple; several firms are listed in the Yellow Pages. However, I don't make a single call. Why should any dealer in the U.K. stock a disk drive for an out-of-date computer that won't run on local current?

"What will we do?" asks Jane.

"It's about nine in the morning in Maine. I'm going to call my parents."

"Good idea."

In two weeks my mother and father are coming to England. They planned their trip last spring at the same time we were planning ours. They have rented a flat in London for three and a half weeks so that they can come and visit us but still retain plenty of freedom. There's much that they want to do in London—my father, longtime sailor, is excited about the Greenwich Observatory; my mother, the horticulturist, wants to visit Kew Gardens; they both want to see *The Mousetrap*. The ring buzzes clearly and my father answers right away, sounding as if he's two towns away. I tell him what has happened and ask if they will pick us up a disk drive for an Apple IIe. He takes down all the model numbers I can give him and says he'll see what he can do. Then my mother comes on the line.

"How are you doing?" she asks. "How's Gardie?" I have written within the last couple of weeks so she knows to ask.

"Not so well," I say. "We'll be glad to see you."

"He's still not eating?"

"Not really."

"Is there anything you want us to bring for him?"

I explain about todays's trip to the commissary with Lisa. "But look. We once got some macaroni and cheese mix in the shape of Teenage Mutant Ninja Turtles. Could you see if your supermarket has them?"

"Goodness. I'll try. And we'll bring some other surprises, too."

"Gardie will be glad to see you. You two may be his best present, surprises or no."

For supper he eats four bites of Kraft macaroni and cheese. He has loved this meal for more than half his life. An hour later he vomits. Jane and I watch Inspector Morse together in silence and then we go to bed.

The next morning, Friday, while I am finishing my notes on *A Laodicean,* which may be Hardy's least-known novel—and deservedly so—the doorbell rings. At the door a Federal Express delivery man hands me a parcel containing the briefcase. I thank him and sign his sheet. As this chimera passes into my hands thirty-nine days after it left them, aside from a slight curiosity to see what all is inside I feel neither pleasure nor relief nor anger nor even irritation, nothing at all, really: but I nonetheless resolve that I will never, ever, send anything via Federal Express.

12

*I*t is the following Tuesday. The
past weekend lightened some; on Sunday morning Gardner ate
two pieces of French toast and kept them down. Then on Sunday afternoon and evening he wept from leg and stomach cramps
before finally going to sleep, and life was dark again. That night
we watched a VCR recording of *48 Hours* we taped the night
before, only to discover that the tape had run out before Eddie
Murphy and Nick Nolte catch the bad guys.

So we decided that this week we'll keep Gardner home from
school to let him recover some strength. On Monday morning we
took him back to the surgery.

This time he saw Dr. Martin, a tall, thin, pleasant man with
a reassuring attitude of common sense. Other than thinness, the
doctor shared none of Gardner's attributes: short, uncooperative,
without a shred of logic. Gardner whined and cried. He refused
to give a urine sample. Jane and I were angry with him. I took
him into the toilet with a specimen jar.

"I won't pee."

"Look. Damn it. How can you get better if you won't let the doctor help you?"

"I won't, Daddy."

I pulled down his sweatpants and underwear and held the jar under his penis. "Here."

"I won't." He started to cry.

We returned with an empty jar. That was my only triumph; I resisted the impulse to fill it with my own urine. Sam was diddling around with some toys on the office floor, a plastic clown, a plastic castle, a plastic telephone with wheels.

"How have his bowel movements been?" I thought for an instant of my grandfather, an early pioneer in pediatrics, who after Harvard in the 1890s went to Vienna to study his specialty. A devotee of Fletcherism, the practice of chewing each bite many times, he was fairly obsessed with bowel regularity. I had no idea when Gardner last had a bowel movement. My grandfather would have been horrified, but how on earth could the boy have any bowel movements at all when no solid food has reached his intestinal tract in nearly two weeks?

"Well, I'll give you a laxative. I don't think there's a blockage, but this will clean him out if there is."

Clean him out? I thought. He's as clean as a swept room. There's nothing inside him at all.

"Do you think it's a virus?" asked Jane. "He hasn't had any temperature."

"Wah." A dispute over the toy castle erupted.

"Let me have that, Sam."

"Stop it, Gardner."

"It could be. Blood testing would tell, but perhaps we should hold off, especially as he's so unhappy right now. However, I do think that if he's not better in a couple of days, he should see a specialist."

The word "specialist" raised for me visions of neurosurgeons and rare-disease immunologists. "Call on Wednesday," he continued. "If there's no change, I'll set you up with a pediatrician in Oxford." In England a "doctor" is a general practitioner; every other physician is a "specialist." I suppose that, strictly speaking, all doctors are specialists—isn't "family medicine" a specialty now?—but I'm not used to hearing the term used that way. Only in a case like, say, Sam's godmother, who works exclusively in neonatal pediatrics, would I think to use the word "specialist" to describe a pediatrician. Or like my grandfather, who practiced when pediatrics was almost unheard of in the United States. The point to remember is that the only way in the British National Health Service one finds a specialist—be it pediatrician or microsurgeon—is through the referral of another physician.

I sense something wrong here, but I can't put my finger on it. It has something to do with the bowel movement question. It sounds like a question out of another era of medicine. But I have no one to wonder with except Jane, and I don't want to add to the stress we are all under. So I keep my mouth shut.

Today I am taking another journey into literary England, specifically to Lyme Regis, the setting for *The French Lieutenant's Woman* and, more to my purposes, the scene of Louisa Musgrove's famous fall in *Persuasion*. Concerned about leaving Jane with both boys in these trying days, I oscillate about going, but take at last a late morning start. At first I retrace my route toward Hampshire down the A34, then turn in the direction of Salisbury. Along the plains that stretch beyond that city I pull off the highway and park in a worn area.

This is Martin Down, a wildflower refuge. I've been told that perhaps three weeks earlier a species of wild orchid, autumn ladies' tresses, *Spiranthes spiralis,* was found in bloom some-where around here. An inconspicuous plant with small blossoms spiraling around a six- or seven-inch spike, it is reported to prefer chalky grasslands, and I can see it should be right at home on Martin Down.

The terrain rolls off to my left as I walk down a dirt road. On my right are hills and swales, all of them surely the products of human activity: large square flat-bottomed depressions fifty feet across and a yard deep, perfectly symmetrical ridges rising thirty feet to a knife-edge at the top, all covered with green. The grass is even, mostly about six inches high. There's no sign of sheep or cows having grazed it though in the fields far in the distance I can see herds of cattle.

I can't think what made this terrain. Chalk mining? The ground by the road is white with the stuff. Prehistoric humans? I know so little about the civilizations that lived in Britain before the Normans, the builders of barrows and henges. There is not a soul nearby to ask.

I don't necessarily expect to see the orchid in flower, but there should be seed pods and possibly a late bloomer. I see a large patch of gorse, a green prickly bush vaguely like juniper with yellow pealike flowers. I know about gorse, or furze, from read-ing. Winnie-the-Pooh fell into a bush of it from the honey tree, and some of Thomas Hardy's characters used to cut it for fuel. Neither activity can have been pleasant, though here and now the plant gives form and color to the landscape.

I cast around for an hour or so, but there's no sign of the ladies' tresses. At first it feels good to be walking about, but after a while the pit of my stomach starts to tighten. I ought to be more productive. I ought to be restoring my family to health. Realizing I cannot find even a dandelion in this mood, I return to the car.

It is well into the afternoon when I roll down into Lyme Regis.

The town is set on the coast like an egg in a nest, surrounded on three sides by hills. I work through narrow, twisted streets, after a bit finding a public car park. The waterfront and main street are still buzzing with people even though it's teatime, the workday winding down. Along the waterfront are video arcades and ice-cream stands. At the western end of the beach, the Cobb—the old stone jetty that creates the harbor—stretches out toward the Channel.

When I read *Persuasion* last month, I copied into my note-book Jane Austen's description of the town: "as there is nothing to admire in the buildings themselves, the remarkable situation of the town, the principal street almost hurrying into the water, the walk to the Cobb, skirting round the pleasant little bay. . . , the Cobb itself, its old wonders and new improvements, with the very beautiful line of cliffs stretching to the east of town, are what the stranger's eye will seek." Today, a century and a half later, these observations endure; she is as accurate as God.

On Broad Street there is a law office bearing a sign:

PYNE HOUSE
This is the most likely
lodging of Jane Austen, whose
visits to Lyme in 1803 and 1804
gave birth to her novel
'Persuasion.'

But nowadays nobody knows her here. It's all honky-tonk, with the arcades and shops and tourists, all Cape Cod or Old Orchard Beach. Jane Austen would hate it. I don't recall the French lieutenant's woman being pleased with Lyme, for that matter.

I stop in a department store across from Pyne House to check on the Hero Turtle card situation. There are none, but I do find a storybook of the four turtles in heroic, if not ninjan, action. The price tag is £5.75. I dig into the pockets of my shorts but can find only coins. Earlier today I had a ten-pound note crumpled in there. Heaven knows where it's gone. I return the book to its shelf and myself to the car, resolving to say nothing of the lost money to Jane, for it will only press her further into whatever slough my son has put her while I've been gone. As the car climbs up the steep hill away from the sea, the sun is hanging low in the sky.

It is almost nine when I return. The boys are in bed, and Jane's lips are thin.

"How was the day?" I ask.

"I didn't know you'd be this late."

"A bad one, eh?"

She starts pulling out plates and silverware for our dinner. All the dishes are washed, another bad sign. "He wept all afternoon. I couldn't stop him. During Sam's nap he wouldn't even watch TV. He wouldn't move off the couch. He just screamed. Sam was good, but after the nap he wanted to go out. I didn't know what to do." She is speaking carefully; right behind her eyes are storms of tears.

"Oh, God, I'm sorry." I consider commiserating by telling her that the trip to Lyme Regis wasn't all that wonderful either, a bit of a bust to tell the truth, but stop myself in time, before a word is out. How can I say any of that after she's spent a day in hell so I could go?

"He just kept crying for you."

"Did he throw up today?"

"No, but he didn't eat anything, either."

Chops, pork or lamb, are broiling in the oven. I try to fill my voice with reason and logic and good sense. "Look. Tomorrow we go back to Dr. Martin. There has to be something more they can do."

121

"I couldn't get him to take his medicine. He screamed so much I just gave up."

"Well, the two of us barely got it down him last night. Anyway, what the hell? A laxative? He doesn't need a goddamn laxative. There's nothing inside him to move."

She takes a tall can of bitter out of the refrigerator and pours two glasses. "I can't believe that seeing a pediatrician is such a big deal."

"Do you think that's the answer?"

"What do you mean?"

"I don't think he's sick." This is the first time I've said this out loud. "Not physically. I think we need a shrink."

"Oh, yes. Of course we do. In fact, we need counseling not just for him but for all of us." I'm listening carefully to the objectivity swelling in her voice. This is not my wife the distraught mother, but my wife the priest, the counselor, who has guided many families through crises worse than this one: desertions, crushing illnesses, suicides, and accidental deaths. "Whatever's making him sick, we're all going to need help to set ourselves right after this blows over. And if it is psychological, we'll all have to work together to make it go away."

We sit down at the table. "Look. I'm sorry I was late. It was a lot farther than I thought. And driving at night is very tough."

She smiles ruefully. "I bet it is. It's just that today was scary. You can't deal with both of them by yourself when he loses it."

Late into the evening we talk, mapping and remapping our territory, going back and forth on the nature and source of Gardner's illness. Virus, bacterial infection, allergy, anger, or grief: we grope in darkness against possibilities we cannot ascertain. Nothing in his past—or our own—has prepared us for this. The one thing clear to us is that the "wait and see" advice we've been getting so far is inadequate. The next morning Dr. Martin agrees with us, confirming for Gardner an appointment on Friday, two days hence, with a Dr. Moncrief, a well-respected pediatrician at the John Radcliffe Memorial Hospital in Oxford. We are moving into the big leagues of the National Health Care system, and not a moment too soon.

13

---

*T*he John Radcliffe Memorial
Hospital is not the same thing as the university's Radcliffe Infirmary. I regularly pass the latter on the Woodstock Road about a quarter mile from the Martyrs' Memorial: an old stone structure set back from the road behind a high stone wall. It was named after a seventeenth-century Oxford doctor who attended William III, and who left behind him the Radcliffe Observatory and the Radcliffe Camera—a library—as well as the Infirmary. I cannot pedal by it without my head filling with images of barbers draining blood into basins, or bearded physicians attaching leeches to consumptive patients.

The John Radcliffe Hospital is something else again. Perched on a hill on the northeast edge of the city just inside the Ring Road, it appears an archetype of The New Hospital: smooth ordered faces of brick and glass surrounded by terrace car parks, canopied admitting area, efficient emergency entrance. As I push Sam up from a low car park at the rear—having dropped Jane and Gardner at the front door—I see a sign requesting public support for a new imaging system the hospital is installing in a wing under construction. The Radcliffe has the reputation as one of the nation's best, balanced on the bright and shining scalpel-sharp cutting edge of Great Britain's medical technology. Looking at the buildings scattered before me, I am breathing easier.

Supplementing my relief is the sense that it's all free, that this wonderful complex sits beneath the vast umbrella of the British National Health Service, and that as a tax-paying resident (for I pay Margaret Thatcher's unpopular poll tax) I am eligible to come in under its sweet shade. One of my colleagues who spent a sabbatical in Cambridge a couple of years ago told me last spring, "The National Health is terrific. They take care of everything." At these words I became so enthusiastic that I immediately asked the business office to remove us from Blue Cross/Blue Shield for our year here, to save the monthly charge of two hundred and fifty-odd dollars.

Sam and I and the stroller ride up an escalator, walk through the cafeteria area, and find a red line in the tile floor, which promises a sign will lead to the Pediatrics Wing. We stroll through a couple of doors and around a corner to find the waiting area. Padded benches surround a large section of padded floor filled with toys and rollicking children, from the center of which rises a blue mountain and falls a yellow slide, both made of a soft material.

"Look, Sam," I say. "Doesn't that look like fun?"

"Yah," he agrees.

He is out of the stroller at once, picking up and sometimes discarding toys, moving through the children toward the slide. I see Jane on a bench reading.

"Where is he?"

"Over there. He's been checked in and weighed. Now we're waiting for Dr. Moncrief."

An hour later we are still waiting, both boys playing happily amid the toys and the slide. Our appointment was set for ten o'clock and it is now well after eleven. For the last few minutes Jane has been standing near a pair of double doors, talking to a woman in a gray suit. Now she calls me over.

"Here's my husband." Turning to me, she says, "Can you get something from Oxford stating you're a student there? A letter?"

What? I think, then speak to the woman. "Well, I'm not registered at the university. I've come here to live for a year as an independent researcher."

The woman is pleasant-faced, on the younger cusp of middle age, with pure gray hair. She cradles a clipboard in the crook of her left arm. "I believe that you will need some student credentials to be eligible for the National Health Service."

With an effort I keep my head. "Really? As a year-long resident, don't I qualify? Our friends who were here last year said they had no trouble."

"Were they full-time students?"

"No, I'm sure their status was the same as mine."

"Well, I don't know. But my understanding is that you need credentials as a student."

"But we live here. We pay the poll tax."

"I'm afraid that has no bearing on your status with National Health."

"Oh, my God."

She sees the horror growing in my face. "Look, I'll call the London office. They can give me the definitive answer. I'll come right back as soon as I find out." She heads off through the doors.

"Can't you get a letter from someone?"

"I can try. It'll take some finagling, but somehow. . . ." My voice trails off. I have discovered that there is a fee for a general admission ticket to attend lectures at Oxford. I have also discovered that it is £500 per term—an exorbitant amount, given that lecturers routinely give permission for visitors to sit in. However, maybe possession of the ticket will give me a booster shot of *bona fides* with the National Health Service.

Then we hear the loudspeaker calling the name of our son. "At last," says Jane.

"You go in. I'll stay here with Sam and wait for the answer from London."

When the woman returns, the news is worse than ever. A letter defining me as a visiting scholar—assuming I could ever get anyone at Oxford to write one for me—is insufficient; I must be enrolled as a full-time student. Otherwise I must live here for a year. In the meantime, we must be considered private patients and must pay for all medical services beyond those provided by the Woodstock Surgery. If Gardner does not improve, we face the prospect of having to hospitalize him without benefit of health insurance.

After she leaves, I bury my face in my hands. This is all my fault. I feel my family walking together on a plank, stepping above waters snapping with hungry sharks, all of England at our backs, and we are utterly alone.

Eventually I gather the younger boy from the slide into my arms and go to find Dr. Moncrief's office, where he and my wife are in conference. Gardner is playing on the floor with a car, quite happy. The doctor is a slim, handsome, elegant man, early fifties perhaps, speaking with a powerful mixture of compassion and common sense. Somehow the office—long and thin, clean and well lit, examining table and scales along one wall and desk at the end, photographs of cheerful animals hanging all about—complements my impression of him.

"Hello."

"This is my husband."

"Hello, Doctor," I say. "I just got through with the National Health representative, and I wanted to let Jane know we do not have coverage."

"Oh no," she says.

"Yes. This shouldn't affect the way you might want to treat him, I suppose, but we might want to consider it when making choices. Are you considering a battery of tests?" My voice, to my ears, at least, carries great calm and self-control.

"As I have been telling your wife," says Dr. Moncrief, "I don't see any evidence of pathology. His tummy is not acute. I can find no swelling to suggest hernia or kidney or appendix or any other sort of blockage. I suspect he's had some kind of virus."

"Even without a fever?" I ask. "He's had a normal temperature, all along."

"He could still have had a virus. Blood testing could reveal whether that is the case. But it is both invasive and expensive—which is a factor, apparently—and honestly, I don't feel it is necessary."

"He's terrified of having blood taken," Jane says.

"Look. He is still well within the ranges of normal weight for his height. He's thin, but he's healthy. I think time will set all this right. However, if you wish, I can give him an ultrasound scan and have some x-rays taken to check his system."

Beyond my panic at finding us suddenly uninsured, I realized that I agree with the doctor: my son's body is healthy, I am sure of it. I do not even believe that there is, or ever has been, a virus.

As if she is reading my mind, Jane speaks. "Could this be a result of stress? What is the possibility of our having him see a psychological counselor?"

Dr. Moncrief looks down the room toward the door, where

the two boys are playing, oblivious to our conversation. "The referral process here is quite lengthy, actually. I'm afraid we are not as quick as we often would like. An appointment with a psychological counselor can take two or three weeks to set up. I can certainly refer you to someone. But I must say that I don't think that will be necessary. I suspect that time will cure whatever is wrong here."

"We certainly hope that's right," says Jane. "But could we ask for a referral right now? If in two weeks we find we don't need it, we can always cancel the appointment. With pleasure." She laughs. "But if in two weeks we find that we do need a counselor, it would be much harder to have to start right from square one."

He considers. "That's a good point. We have a fine child psychiatrist on the staff. She is away this week, but I'll speak to her about you when she returns."

Comfort is beginning to return, and with it, optimism. We will be able to find help here at the John Radcliffe, and somehow we will be able to pay for it. As we leave, we agree to keep in touch with Dr. Moncrief through Dr. Martin at the surgery. I look for the woman from the National Health to pay her the £15 for this visit, but she is nowhere in sight. No matter. Most certain of all, optimism or no, we will be billed.

By evening two events have occurred to raise our hopes higher. First, in the afternoon I telephoned my school, asking that I be reinstated immediately in Blue Cross/Blue Shield. The secretary pulled my file. "I don't see that you were ever terminated from the program," she said, and my heart leaped, soared like a bird. Never before had I felt so grateful to an institution for making a mistake, for not following my directions. "I'll double-check," she continued, "but I think you're fine. Would you like me to send some forms to make out-of-state claims?"

"Oh, yes. And can you send a booklet describing what's covered?" And I thanked her all the way from the bottom of my feet.

Now at supper Gardner—deciding he's hungry, praise God— has requested Chinese food, chicken and snow peas, Peking dumplings. He hasn't been vomiting as much this week as last, only fasting, as if his mind has decided that, if he doesn't put it down, he won't throw it back up. As a defensive strategy, this is Pyrrhic, for it can only lead to ultimate defeat. We know we have to get him eating again.

So I joyfully hop on my bicycle and race to the Coop grocery, where I find in the frozen food rack a dinner of chicken, peas, and mushrooms. We serve it to him on rice, with soy sauce, and it suffices; he eats it all. Afterward he asks for mint chip ice cream. Again I pedal to the Coop, and he eats two bowls of the awful green stuff I bring back. He goes to bed happy, and he does not vomit. "He is risen, he is risen," sings my heart, as we settle down to our own lamb chops and broccoli in front of Inspector Morse.

It is two days later, Saturday, and we are driving west on the M4, an eight-lane high-speed motorway. Rain is sluicing out of the gray skies, but the British drivers gun through it, simply another day at the speedway. I am holding tight to the left lane at sixty-five miles an hour, the slowest driver on the road. Past me on the right stream the other cars.

By now the floating balloon of Thursday's elation has deflated considerably. We have not been cured, despite the big dinner. Yesterday's voice was whiny and fretful, its food a single bowl of cornflakes. Today, determined to have fun despite the rain, we are heading to the "International Art of Lego Exhibit" at The Exploratory, a children's museum in Bristol.

Lego are small plastic blocks with little nubs on top, bright yellow and blue and red and green and white and black and gray. The nubs allow them to be snapped together to build, as far as I can see, damned near anything: buildings, creatures, vehicles, small worlds. The company has designed accessories—wheels, antennae, windscreens, canopies, little Lego people—so that children can build petrol stations, space colonies, pirate ships, knights' castles. There is a junior version of Lego—Duplo—larger and simpler for two-to-four-year-olds; in consequence Gardner has been working in the Lego medium for nearly four years, or two-thirds of his life. This trip is a bit like taking the young Mozart to a recital of sonatas.

Both boys are subdued, depressed as much by the grim weather and the drive as by anything else, since we began the day with enthusiasm and good spirit. We work our way into Bristol, a large city set on the estuary of the River Severn, on the opposite bank of which lies Wales. Another motorway, the M32, leads us right into the city center, and we find The Exploratory easily. I drop the others at the door and go off to park the car.

Once I return, we join the crowds looking around at the museum's permanent exhibits. The building was once a train station, and it still has the lofty dark warehouse-like look of its ancestry. Set out for the public are displays of electricity, bubbles, wave motion—in short, the warp and weft of children's science museums. I carry Sam on my shoulders, while Gardner moves slowly along with Jane. From underneath, I sense that Sam is enjoying everything greatly, even though he can't do much more than push an occasional button and wonder at the response. Both children are interested but passively so, unable to interact with the exhibits because of lack of development in one case, of energy in the other.

The Art of Lego is upstairs at the back end of The Exploratory, and getting Gardner up there is an effort. By now his strength has run out. He has become peevish and tenuous. We jolly him up the stairs, where we find a series of display cases and beyond a number of large sculptures. I set Sam free on the floor and tell Gardner, "Just go wherever you want. After this, we'll go down to the room where you can build your own stuff."

Along one wall is a history of Lego, describing its development by a Scandinavian toymaker who has clearly passed a bonanza onto his sons, the present owners. The big idea was to create a toy that did not become obsolete when supplemented with more sophisticated elements. I think of the basic Lego set Gardner began with, and the theme sets of knights and spacemen he has begun to acquire, and the ones with motors waiting for him in the future. To consider the number of bricks required by all the other Lego builders in the world—if Gardner is representative—is to consider the distance to the stars.

Other displays near the door are scientific and not Legotic, if that is the word: a nuclear power source model, a mock-up of geological strata. Then I come to the sculpture. Old King Cole, with pipe, bowl, and fiddlers three, stands about four feet high, made entirely of Lego. Several abstract pieces twirl and twinkle on walls or in cases. There is a Lego picnic lunch laid out, a Lego throne for anyone to sit on, and a life-sized Lego organ and organist. The skin of the human figures is made of Lego yellow, giving them the rather startling aspect of all suffering from serious jaundice, but on the whole the pieces are more startling in their flexibility. The artists' ability to surpass the limits of rectangularity astounds me. Every time I try to build something with Gardner's Lego, the result has corners, whether it's a house or a human. These creatures curve, somehow. I wonder, did the artists use glue? They must have.

Suddenly I see Gardner sitting on the floor under one of the displays, knees together and legs splayed, gazing toward the center of the room at nothing in particular, sucking his thumb. He looks lost, like a rowboat adrift in a gray flat empty ocean.

"How's it going?" I squat beside him.

After a long pause, he answers. "O.K."

"Do you like these things? Pretty cool, huh?"

"Yeah." But there is no enthusiasm, no expression at all in his voice. He seems exhausted.

"You ready to go downstairs?"

"O.K."

Downstairs he revives somewhat. Boxes and boxes of Lego and Duplo materials have been laid down in the center of the long room, with thirty or so children rooting away in them and snapping the bright blocks together. Around the walls is a child-high shelf on which the fruits of all this labor is displayed. Above each piece is pinned a slip of paper bearing the signature—or mark, if literacy has not yet been mastered—of the artist and the time of day. After two hours or so the art is dismantled and recycled.

His competitive urge surfaces and he makes three separate constructions for display: a plane, a control tower, and a G.I. Joe piece of field artillery. He builds with intensity and concentration, but without much patience; complaints quickly arise if a needed part is not instantly available. Sam works in the Duplo medium, having a fine time.

We leave about twelve-thirty, and stop within the city limits at a Burger King. It is very crowded and very slow, fast food

---

apparently something of an oxymoron in Great Britain. He eats three bites of a cheeseburger and falls asleep during the ride home. Although the rain has stopped, the skies remain gray, and as I drive along I wonder without the slightest glimmer of irony whether or not he believes he has had a good day.

14

*T*oday is Monday, October 1, the day Jane says, "White rabbit," and I "Rabbit-rabbit," to bring good luck for the coming month. The first sounds of the day, of the month for that matter, are moans and weeping from Gardner's room. My watch reads 6:12 as Jane leads him into our room, supporting him like a very little, very old man. He is inconsolable.

"What's the matter, bud?" I ask as she lifts him into the middle of the bed.

The weeping seems to rise out of him like springwater, deep and cold and sourceless, unstoppable. "Ohhh-anngh," he sobs.

"Gardner," says Jane. "Use words. Tell us what the trouble is."

"Ohhh-anngh!"

"Please, Gardie. Use words." The familiar instruction of his day-care center back in Massachusetts, to combat the infant id out of control: "Don't hit, don't grab, don't cry—use your words."

And then like a miracle he ceases, clamps down on it, save for those little gasps we all puff out when we stop crying, and he

says in a trembling, tear-roughened voice: "I want to go home."
He pauses. "Ohhh-anngh!"

He has never said this before, at least where I could hear
him. It hits me how much he really knows. He knows he's stuck
here, and he knows he hates it. He knows how important this
year is for both me and Jane. Most important of all, he knows
the power of language, the frightful magic inherent in the act of
naming, and my heart shrinks at how difficult, even how danger-
ous he believes it is for him to confront his two parents directly, to
put this desire upon his tongue. Oh, please, Jesus, I pray, please
let us stay, as at the same time I sit on the panic starting to wash
over and through me.

"But, Gardner, this is our home," says Jane. "For this year."

"Ohhh-anngh!"

"Look," I say. "It's your home, too. Let's try to think of ways
we can make it more fun for you."

He turns silent, and I press my advantage. "What would make
England a better home for you to live in?"

From the other bedroom across the hall comes, "Momma."
Jane rises.

"I don't know." His voice is that of a Very Small Creature.

"Well, let's think about it."

"Greg and Scott?"

Damn. "Well, they can't be in England, I'm afraid. But you
have some friends here. Pete Brown. Alistair. Isn't there anything else?"

"I miss Chazzie."

Jane returns with Sam in her arms.

Chaz was a large enthusiastic shepherd-labrador we had for
the first three years of Gardner's life until he was killed by a car.
I can think of a dozen reasons for not getting a dog while we

are living in Hereford House, but not one for articulating any of them at this moment. "A dog? That's a thought."

"Yay," says Sam. "Goggie. Woof. Woof."

At breakfast Gardner is whining for blueberry muffins, an impossibility. I walk across the street to the old railway embankment and return in five minutes with a small pan of blackberries.

"How about these?"

"Oh, yes, yes, yes."

Jane makes a batch of wholemeal bramble muffins. As soon as they are cool enough to eat she butters one for him. He eats it enthusiastically. Five minutes later, he vomits.

In Woodstock two streets turn west from the A34 to converge into one at the Bear Hotel, the road afterward leading to the main entrance to Blenheim Palace. On the triangle thus formed sits most of the town's business district. Walking down one street we pass the Coop, the chemist, a print shop, Mr. Freeman's butcher shop, the Woodstock Turf Accountants, the antiquarian bookshop; down the other, the greengrocer, two gift shops, the post office. Along the stretch toward the palace gates are St. Mary Magdalene's, Martyn Brown's museum, Barclay's Bank, and the Blenheim Tea Room, where television's Miss Marple did a bit of sleuthing in *Nemesis*. Into this commercial microcosm has arrived today a street fair, and in the late afternoon we all stroll down to try it out.

Compared to the St. Giles Fair, this is a duck pond, though it has plenty to keep us entertained. Both streets are closed to automotive traffic, filled as they are with rides and games and food stalls. Two small automobile carousels have entranced Sam. "We came here on our walk this morning. They weren't open, but he sat in them anyway, happy as a lamb," says Jane. Now that they're moving, he won't leave them. Gardner is wandering around staring at the dart booths and other games of skill, hoping to win anything with a Teenage Mutant Hero Turtle on it. His spirits have improved during the day. He finds one booth that awards prizes with liberality and spends a couple pounds prying loose from it a pair of swim goggles, two plastic swords, and a squirt gun.

Just as we are turning toward home, he meets a classmate from the Woodstock Primary School, Alistair Wallworth, and his parents. The two boys admire each other's loot, while the adults chat. I am pleased to see how enthusiastic my son seems, but then I feel something beneath my heel and look down to discover my watch has a broken strap and I have stepped on it, breaking the crystal.

Today is Wednesday, my mother's birthday as it happens. She and my father have just arrived in London, and we all will celebrate Friday night when they come up for the weekend. Gardner—whose spirits have been gaining altitude over the past two days—has returned to school after a week and two days of absence. It was not a success; leg cramps and wails and tears were our companions while he, Sam, and I walked over. Somehow I pried free of clutching fingers and got away. Jane has headed into Oxford to pick up a lecture list from the theology department. Lectures start next week. I have seen the English list, with lectures on John Donne, Charles Dickens, and my present reading subject, Thomas Hardy. I have recently finished *Far From the Madding Crowd* with much pleasure, and while Sam fiddles about, I am sitting with him out in the garden coming to the end of one of Hardy's oddest novels, the last one he published, *The Well-Beloved*.

A sculptor named Jocelyn Pierston, who grows up on "The Isle of Slingers"—really the Isle of Portland, fifteen miles south of Dorchester—successively falls in love with three generations of women: mother, daughter, granddaughter, each when about twenty, all named Avice. Pierston develops a theory of beauty, that the principle of Aphrodite, Astarte, Friegda—the goddesses of love—inhabits a particular body for a time, an incarnation he refers to as the "Well-Beloved." The Avices are all such embodiments, of course, as well as other women in the book.

It's a shallow theory, permitting Pierston great sexual freedom and demanding of him no great responsibility. But suddenly it occurs to me that this book is not about love at all, not even lust; it is time that consumes Hardy here. The successive Avices shelter Pierston from the necessity of recognizing advancing age. He can remain a perpetual adolescent, sheltered in a time warp with the same sweetheart reappearing every twenty years as an emblem of his undying youth. I am reminded somehow of Dorian Gray, although there the portrait changes while the youth remains untouched. The procession of Well-Beloveds become magic mirrors in which Pierston—a quintessential narcissist—may admire his own unchanging reflection.

The inability to deal with the movement of time signals dysfunction and, at its extreme limit, insanity. The maddest lover in Dickens's collection of loonies is Miss Havisham, who stopped all the clocks and wore her wedding dress for the rest of her life after her Well-Beloved, Compeyson, deserted her. Time is in one sense change, movement—of clock hands, of human feet, of all our lives and deaths—and when the power fails us to rejoice in its passage, or at least to take notice of it, the world grows increasingly dark and distorted. This meditation has moved some distance from *The Well-Beloved* until gradually I see it is focused directly on my son.

About two o'clock Jane returns from Oxford with packages. "I went to the open market near the bus station."

"What did you get?"

She tips her head in slight embarrassment. "Some stuff for Gardner. *Robocop* and *E.T.* A couple of knights. I thought we could put *E.T.* away for another time, when we need it. But he's been asking for *Robocop*." Back home I taped *Robocop* when it was broadcast on one of the networks, and he and I would watch it together. Some of the violence was pretty horrific, but we fast-forwarded through it and reveled side-by-side as the brave and honorable Murphy, brought back from the dead and transformed into a futuristic knight in armor, tilted away at dreadful dragons named Clarence Boddicker and Dick Jones.

An hour later Gardner is home from school. It has been a good day, apparently, and he is further elated by all the booty. We settle down to watch *Robocop* just like the old days. Unfortunately, not long into the tape, it becomes clear that the version we have at home has been edited for television, and the one we have here is more violent than ever. There's nothing for it but to punch the fast-forward button and blitz through the bad stuff to get to the good; and in our robot voices we recite with Murphy the Robocop his prime directives: "SERVE THE PUBLIC TRUST. PROTECT THE INNOCENT. UPHOLD THE LAW."

Today, Thursday morning, begins with the worst of the before-school symptoms—whining, fasting, balking. Just beyond the gate, leg cramps hit with astonishing force, so that he drops to the pavement writhing and weeping, tearing his lunch bag in the process. He and Jane burst together through the door like a pair of cyclones, scattering Sam and me out of their paths like leaves. Leg cramps forgotten, he races to his bedroom, Jane at his heels.

"You won't do anything," she tells him. "You won't take medicine, you won't brush your teeth. You won't go to school or to the doctor. You won't eat. It always has to be your way."

"I don't care."

"Look at all these toys. They don't make any difference, do they?"

"I don't care," is his tear-choked refrain as she, filled with equal portions of fury and fear, takes away all the bribes of the last few days: both plastic swords, new Lego from Bristol, and *Robocop*. Then she leaves him in his room, where he snuffles himself, after a bit, to sleep. Still smoldering, she departs with Sam for a walk through the palace grounds.

I spend the morning trying to read Hardy's first published novel, *Desperate Remedies*, while Gardner sleeps upstairs. A wonderfully cinematic scene opens the story: a young woman named Cytherea Graye is sitting at a community Shakespeare presentation; bored, she gazes idly out a small window to a church spire across the way. She sees several workmen on scaffolding, one of whom she recognizes as her father, an architect in charge of the repairs. As she watches in horror, he stumbles and plunges out of view; then, to the astonishment of those around her who have seen nothing of this, she shrieks and falls to the floor.

Such an image of the isolation of the soul in torment! What window has my son been looking through, what has he seen there, that sets him writhing and weeping in the street?

Is this year being written by Thomas Hardy?

In the afternoon I watch him lie quietly on the couch. I see how his body has grown thinner and thinner, wasting away under the gazes of his parents as if we are withering suns.

"Dad," he says in his voice of reasoned conciliation, The Diplomat, "can I watch TV now?"

I hate this. I hate to say no. Jane and I have discussed how to handle his television privileges when he doesn't go to school, but for now I temporize. "What did your mother say?" She is out again strolling Sam around the palace park.

"Oh, yeah." He is all rational consideration. "She said not while school was in session. Is school in session right now?"

I raise my wrist to look at my watch, but of course it isn't there. The day after I stepped on it, I searched through Woodstock and found a combination sweater-and-jewelry shop across from the chemist. The owner has assured me he can obtain a crystal, and I will be able to pick it up tomorrow. So now I bluff it. "Yup. Sorry. Another half hour and you can watch."

"That's O.K., Dad. There's probably nothing on now, anyhow."

He lies on the couch with his legs drawn up to his chest, a blanket trailing from his hand to the floor. He is sucking his thumb, his head twisted sideways, and he gazes out toward the wall into the middle distance. The index finger of the hand he is sucking is moving slowly, hypnotically, against the satin edge of his blanket. On the low table in front of him is a mixing bowl. Narrowly I study him, watching the gentle rising and falling of his arm across his chest.

"Hey. Gramma and Grampa are coming tomorrow."

"I know that."

"Sure. Do you want to help me make a pie for them?"

He does not look up at me, but continues his thumb sucking, his satin stroking, his wall watching. "No thanks, Dad."

His face is beautiful, what I can see of it. Translucent skin has drawn tight across his cheeks. His eyes seem to have enlarged, so that even in this dreamy droop-lidded condition he presents an ethereal, angelic aspect. His nose has become thinner, sharper, bringing definition and punctuation to what used to be soft childish features. My heart shrinks in the face of this face.

I speak, unable to stop myself. "Say. Would you like a snack?" But I know, have known for weeks, what he is going to say.

"No thanks, Dad."

A couple hours pass. "Dad," he calls from the living room. The strollers have not yet returned, and I am baking. He has not watched television at all this afternoon, only stared at the blank screen and dozed. "Will you carry me upstairs?" This request, which has been coming more frequently in recent days, is made in the Young Patient voice.

"Can't you go up yourself?" I respond in pom-pom tones, trying to keep cheer and enthusiasm at the forefront, although I can feel resentment and fear crowding behind them.

"No. I can't, Daddy."

I scoop him up and carry him from the couch up the stairs to his room, where I deposit him on his mattress. I barely allow myself to notice how easy this task has been; he has become a Hollow Man, made of dried twigs and straw.

"Dad. I have to pee."

"O.K.," I reply. "Come on into the bathroom."

"Will you carry me?"

Irritation—if that's what it is—floods me. "Come on. You certainly can walk in here."

"I *can't*."

"Goddamn it." Filled with purpose, I stride into his room and lift him from his bed in a smooth clean-and-jerk. Back in the bathroom I set him on the floor next to the tub. "There you are."

He lies there, working his sweatpants and his Ninja Turtle underpants down his legs, jerkily, like a mechanical toy. Then in his plaintive babyish voice he asks, "Will you hold me up so I can pee?"

"No," I say. "You stand up. You aren't that weak."

"I *can't*."

"Listen. You are ruining this year. I've been waiting for this year. I won't ever have another. You are wrecking it."

His eyes are huge. "Help me."

"Goddamn it." My voice is getting louder, and my chest tighter. "You stand up."

"I can't, Daddy."

"Goddamn you," I say, and I hear my voice, as from a distance, shouting. "If you can't stand up, then you go ahead and pee all over yourself. See if I care."

He looks up at me, his eyes wide before my anger, and then urine arcs from his penis and splashes across his body, his clothes, and the floor.

"Goddamn you," I shout and jerk him from the floor. He makes no sound. "How dare you do that?" I sit on the side of the tub and, oblivious to the wetness staining the legs of my trousers, turn him over my knees and slap five times his naked upturned buttocks—all the time wondering in some quieter part of my mind whether or not for this act of violence God or my son or my wife or anyone else, not least of all I myself, will ever be able to forgive me.

15

*T*oday, Friday, my parents are coming up from London. This week they arrived at a flat near Paddington Station for three weeks, not only to see us, but also to explore London and some of the rest of the country for themselves. Although my mother has visited here several times, my father has not. A naval aviator during World War II, he flew all over Central and South America, but never until now has he crossed either the Atlantic or the Pacific. When the London idea was first broached, while Jane and I were still making our own plans for the year, we encouraged it cheerfully. I was eager to have them see us happy in a foreign land.

Now I'm looking forward to their arrival with some desperation. Both boys are fond of them, and more and more Jane and I have been counting on their presence to turn Gardner around, restore his spirits, set him back at the table.

Somehow we have revived from yesterday's debacle, despite a horrible dull ache above and behind my stomach that I can almost at times forget. I managed to get Gardner through the wet gray morning to school. He was subdued along the way, but there were no leg cramps; and although he entered the building sluggishly, there were no tears, either. Mrs. Tattam tells us that he recovers quite quickly after being left, even when the weeping is most violent, and that he is usually lethargic and passive, but not difficult, not even particularly unhappy.

At 10:30 I drive in to meet the train. I'm still a little nervous driving—I always say to myself, "Now, remember, you're in England, idiot," before I turn on the motor. Starting out on a small empty road is where the worst danger lies, I've been told; with nothing around to establish the context of keeping to the left, an American can easily slip into old habits. Once traffic appears, flowing on all sides, then ambiguity evaporates, orientation returns, and the proper choices become clear. The seven roundabouts on the A34 into Oxford revolve past, and soon I'm spinning down Woodstock Road, which becomes St. Giles—site of the big fair—turning right at the Ashmolean Museum on Beaumont Street, left on Worcester, right on Park End; and up on the right the station appears with the red-on-white British Rail logo, a pair of horizontal parallel lines cut by a zig-zag line to form arrows, the top pointed right, the bottom left:

I arrive just as the train does. My parents look fit and happy as they enter the station. I hurry up to my bag-burdened father to relieve him of some of the load. "Hi, there. Let me help."

"Hey," he says grinning. "I'll be some glad to get rid of that thing." It is a heavy bag with the Apple logo on it—the disk drive that we hope will get the computer working.

"Hey, Ma." She smiles and holds her arms out for a hug. "It's good to see you."

"How are you, dear boy?"

"O.K. But it's been a bit rough lately."

They know Gardner has been having trouble, but the last letter I sent them contained news now nearly two weeks old. Times have changed. My heart is full of last night, of last week; but I can't say it now, and anyway they should see for themselves.

"He's not settled in yet?" my mother asks.

"No," I say grimly. "We can't get him to eat."

Back at Hereford House we move my parents onto the second floor, where they will have a brightly lit room and a shower, to boot. My father and I waste no time hooking the new disk drive to the computer. I put in the word processing program, snap the switch, and the familiar humming and clicking occur. Then, magic, the AppleWriter logo appears, followed by the computer's version of a clean piece of paper: a blank screen with the data line across the top. I type, "Now is the time," and the cursor flies across the screen, leaving the letters behind it like tracks. I put in a disk of old files and load one of them, any one, into the machine. The new drive whirs and my old words flash onto the screen.

"Eureka! Thank heavens! We're in business." I turn to my father. "Thanks, Dad." It is the first triumph in some time.

"You're welcome. As I said, I'm awfully glad to get that damned thing off my hands. There were moments it weighed a ton."

"Well, then, I'm glad for your sake too that your efforts weren't for naught."

Downstairs we all rejoice in this small victory and chat around the topic of Gardner until three o'clock when we all troop over to the school to pick him up. He is overjoyed to see his grandparents, whom we introduce to Mrs. Tattam. Then we all tour the school.

My father is a wonderful storyteller, who always brought home a hilarious cast of Maine characters from work. I inherited a love of lore and language from him—tall tales, anecdotes, stories from the shipyard where he was plant engineer—but when the conversation gets personal, he often turns silent and reflective, or sometimes, almost oratorical. He was overwhelmed, my mother told me, when he learned that his first grandson had been named after him—although he never explicitly told us so. Indeed, he used to say that "Gardner" was a cross of a name to bear, a source of teasing when he was young, and all his life he has been known as "Bill." Still, the common name has created a bond between them. Last summer they went out mackerel fishing, the two Gardners, one four, the other seventy, their rods dipping together over the side of the Boston Whaler in the gentle swells. They returned from the sea joyfully bitching about the lack of fish. This time, however—because of my father's reticence in speaking of stressful matters close to him—the bond creates additional stress; and as my parents begin to get a sense of the scope of our problem, I can see him unhappily pulling into himself.

Yet Gardner is happy and excited to see his grandparents. Unfortunately he has so little energy that he can no longer express his pleasure as he used to. Back at Hereford House he wants only to lie down on the couch for television. My mother, Jane, and Sam go for a walk on the Blenheim grounds, while my father and I stay behind. Outside in the garden, I cautiously approach the problem with him.

"Well. What do you think about Gardie?"

He does not answer immediately. "He seems quiet. I can see he's thinner."

"We're hoping that you can cheer him up some. He has been very sad. It has been hard."

"I imagine."

"The other day he said he wanted us to get a dog. I don't know what to do."

It's clear he has no answers—who does?—so we talk about other things, my sister, friends back in Maine, the flat in London. When the others get home, Jane prepares a birthday dinner for my mother: roast chicken, peas, rice, cranberry preserves. The Blenheim Palace gift shop sells wine with a Blenheim label, a nice Bordeaux, which provides a moment of glee and a pleasant period of sipping. For dessert I have made (what else?) a blackberry pie with my mother's initials on it.

Gardner eats tangible amounts of chicken and cranberry and then goes to sleep on the couch. When we carry him upstairs, leg cramps and tears fall on him with a fury, and Jane and I in turn massage his back and legs and feet for forty-five minutes before he quiets down.

Afterward, my parents in bed above us all, we two watch a movie, *Witness*, about a small Amish boy named Samuel—"His name is El," just like Sam—who witnesses a murder in Philadelphia and then is forced to flee with his mother Kelly McGillis and policeman Harrison Ford back to the Amish community to hide from the bad guys. In the city Samuel is interested but alien, at great risk from forces he neither controls nor understands. His luminous eyes haunt me, remind me despite his name of my older son's. Kelly McGillis is awkward and ungainly in Philadelphia, but warm and lovely in her spare clean home. Harrison Ford—whose character is like me named John, "God is gracious," John Book (should my name be John Book?)—tries to enter into the Amish world. Oh, he plays his forbidden radio and fixes his forbidden car, but still all the time he wants to please and love Samuel and his mother, wants to help with the community barn building, wants oh so much to belong.

We are awakened around six o'clock with weeping and complaints of an aching stomach, which are soothed by Saturday morning cartoons and a piece of French toast—a request made and granted even though everyone else is having pancakes to go with the maple syrup my parents brought from Maine. Today the Woodstock Primary School is having a fair of its own—used toys and clothes, tables of local crafts, a bake sale, a boot sale. This last has nothing to do with footwear; people drive into the school's car park, open their trunks—called "boots" here—and sell used items from them. By noon all of Hereford House has come to the fair. Jane has found a Woodstock Primary School sweatshirt for my sister's birthday next week and for £2.00 a used MASK fighter, a foot-long plastic aircraft, combination jet and helicopter, twin of a toy Gardner left in Massachusetts. My mother has bought a maroon plaid outdoor vest for Sam and a WPS sweatshirt for Gardner. Sam loves his vest, will not have it removed, and Gardner—to our astonishment—wears the sweatshirt happily, though we cannot believe that he is signaling a change of heart about the school itself. My father and I take turns buying and distributing sausages and what pass for hot dogs from a charcoal grill outside. The boys wander around, Sam in his vest wide-eyed and slack-jawed in wonder, Gardner in his sweatshirt growing tired and downcast and sullen.

Then later in the afternoon the Browns come over for tea. The adults sit around the small table in the living room as Jane brings out a pot, cups, milk, sugar, and some tarts my mother bought at the school fair. My father is chatting up Jane Brown, charmed by her as I knew he would be; he is a courtly man, an old knight-at-arms with many tales to tell, and her vivacity lights him up in an instant. My mother and Martyn hit it off as well, his diffident smile warming through his beard, her head cocked to the side with pleasure. I begin to pour the tea.

"Where's Gardner?" says Peter from the door. Sam and Harriet are playing outside.

"I think he's upstairs," says Jane.

"Can I play with his toys?"

"Ask him. I'll bet he'll let you."

He disappears. Shortly afterward Gardner enters, silent, stoop-shouldered, wan and sullen, to take a seat beside Jane on the couch.

"Did Pete find you?" she asks.

"Yes. I told him he could play with my new toys."

"That was nice of you. Don't you want to play, too?"

"No, thank you."

For a time he remains there snuggled against his mother, impassive as a stone. It's hard to say if he inhibits the conversation substantially—he is, after all, small and tucked to the side—but he is a distinct substance against which it occurs.

"Mommy," he says at last, "I would like some chicken dinner now."

The adults do not all fall into an immediate hush, but it's clear that everyone has heard this remark.

"It's not yet five. You boys will be eating in an hour or so."

"I'm not eating with you guys?"

"No, the grown-ups are eating later."

He screws up his face to howl—by now all pretense of adult confabulation has ground to a halt—but before he can emit a sound, she stands. "Come with me."

Out on the stairs their discussion is audible, Jane's voice talking reasonably away in counterpoint with his, which whines and cries in soft spurts of unreasonable desire. Then he retreats upstairs, Peter by this time having removed the MASK Fighter and probably the Teenage Mutant Hero Turtles—who can surely pilot such a plane—to the garden. The tea party continues.

In the early afternoon of the next day, Sunday, I drive my parents to Oxford, across from the Ashmolean Museum where they can pick up the Oxford Tour. In the morning Jane and my mother went to church in Wootton, while my father and I stayed home with the boys. My father attends church very rarely, my mother often; he was pleased to take Sam for a walk and let me stay home coping with Gardner, who sat lethargically in front of the television.

The night before we had finally discussed his behavior with my parents. We described the progress of his time in England—especially since school had started—and the medical assistance we had sought. "The doctors don't know what's wrong with him," Jane said. "They just keep saying, 'Wait and see.'"

"What else can we do?" I asked. I did not describe the urination scene in the bathroom two days earlier.

My mother demurred, but my father was moved. "He's jerking your chains," he said, and my heart fell. "Did you see him eating tonight? He can eat, if he wants to." It was true that Gardner had eaten reasonably well that evening, and my mind conjured up the other instances they have seen this weekend of his manipulation: the French toast, the tears and cramps at bedtime, the interruption of tea with a demand for his own dinner. "You can't keep catering to him." Jane might have been struck in the face by his words, for she looked about to throw something or to burst into tears or both, but I knew that he was acutely aware of and

152

responsive to our pain, speaking—with difficulty, for as I have said he does not deal easily with his own family's traumas—in an attempt to help, to offer something, to try somehow to stop the hemorrhaging. And yet I knew too that he was wrong, that ever since Thursday it had been made clear that nothing I could do would make my son eat, or make him go happily to school, or make him smile with joy in this foreign world.

At the last roundabout coming into Oxford, as I let out the clutch, I feel a slippage. This has happened once or twice before, but I don't want to think about it now. We pass the old Radcliffe Infirmary, and soon I pull into a parking place just up from the corner of Beaumont and the Ashmolean. They get out of the Maxi, and I hand them their small overnight bags. "Well, thank you," says my mother. "I hope things improve. Will we see you next week?"

"Yes. Jane has a conference next Saturday. He and I will try to come down to London on Sunday. As long as I think he can do it. Are you far from the station?"

"No," says my father. "Three blocks. Just call us."

"Ring us up," says my mother smiling, ever alert to the differences between English and American. "As we say."

"Oh, and John," says my father. "Please. For God's sake, don't get a dog."

16

*I*t's Tuesday morning and Lisa and I are once again headed out to the air base to search for food for my son and a birthday present for her husband. It's a good trade: Jane is sitting with Sam and Lisa's son Jordan, I'm driving her twenty miles for her errand, and she's getting us Froot Loops and Corn Pops. We turn left on the A4095.

"So he was glad to see your parents?"

"Who knows? I think so. But the beat goes on. Yesterday he threw up at lunch again at school."

"Poor little boy."

"That was the first time in a week. But he didn't come home. He stayed for the rest of the day."

She pauses. Her pleasant optimism appreciates something to be grateful for. Then she asks, "What are the doctors saying? Have you been lately?"

"Jane took him to see Dr. Martin yesterday. I like him, a very nice man."

"Uh-huh," she agrees.

"He still doesn't think it's anything. We heard about some kids at the primary school with a bacterial infection—you know, they were vomiting, couldn't keep their food down, sound familiar?— so Jane asked him if we could try a course of antibiotics. You know, last year, whenever Sam got a cold, he had a standing order at our local CVS for antibiotics because of ear infections. All we did was ask for it. Here, they act like it should be used only on the dead and dying."

"Yeah, I know. But things may be a bit loose in the States. Lots of doctors overmedicate, I think."

Although I agree with her, I'm not sure what the chiropractic bias is toward medication—conservative, I bet—and I suspect this is party line. "Well, Jane asked if we could try a course of antibiotics, so in case it's bacterial we can fix it. He said he'd think about it."

"Good." After a minute she says, "By the way. We would like to have you folks over for Thanksgiving dinner. I know it's a long ways away now, but it would be nice to have you."

A festival dedicated to the eating of American food: Thanksgiving floods me with both joy and despair as I consider all the Thanksgivings from my past, and all the signs of how this one will turn out. Still I am moved by her generosity and kindness. "What a wonderful invitation. Thank you so much. I'll talk to Jane about it. I hope we can have Gardner on track by then."

"I'm sure you will."

At a light I turn right onto the secondary road toward Heyford. As I accelerate, I feel the clutch slipping. "Feel that?" I ask.

Lisa knows cars. "You got clutch trouble."

"I know. I'm taking it into Mr. Young's tomorrow. Argh. It won't be cheap."

The narrow road swings down a hill. Near the bottom we stop at a red light guarding a single-track bridge. I say, "Yesterday morning I biked into Oxford for my first lectures."

"Oh? How were they?"

"Good." But she is not literary, and I don't pursue it. We turn silent as the English countryside slides by. Another thing I don't mention is a conversation I had with Jane yesterday after I returned from Oxford. We were standing outside, Sam sitting on the wall watching for goggies to pass by. He is a fixture on the wall, well known to many shoppers at the store next door, a tiny Humpty Dumpty waving to all the king's doggies. Jane was describing the trip to school and the call saying that Gardner had vomited again.

"They said he seemed okay, and then asked if I wanted him to stay, and I said yes."

Thoughts of the last few days washed over me like effluent. "Goddamn it. He is just destroying this year. Just destroying it."

She did not respond.

"Goggie," remarked Sam, and sure enough, one walked by with its owner.

"Hello," we said.

"Hello. Hello, Sam," said the woman.

"Goggie."

After she went into the shop, I said, "Well, all I can say is, if we have to go home because of him, we are going to need a hell of a lot of counseling. Because I am never going to be able to forgive him for ruining this year."

After Lisa and I return, Kelloggsed and Krafted and Oscar Mayered, I climb on my bicycle to trek into Oxford. All the English literature lectures are given in St. Cross Hall, so I ride past Blackwell's on Broad Street and straight on down Holywell to St. Cross Street. I am still trying to understand how the Oxford University educational process works; it seems far more arcane—and casual, for that matter—than, say, cricket.

When students apply to the university, they request membership in one of several colleges, usually chosen because of interest. Some colleges are noted for a particular discipline, as Corpus Christi is for classics. Other applicants make their request because of prestige or public school connection, though this seems to be a dying practice. Yet for my part I know that, if by some miracle I might become an Oxford undergraduate, I would wish only to be a member of Balliol, simply because that was Lord Peter Wimsey's college. Subsequently a position is offered in a college, which may or may not be the applicant's choice.

Undergraduates eat and sleep in their colleges. They do not study a more or less broad curriculum the way most American undergraduates do; instead they *read,* limiting themselves to one or two academic disciplines. A tutor, that is, a faculty member associated with the college, meets with each student to assign or "set" paper topics, which are a week later discussed, criticized, and defended. All of this work is directed toward passing written examinations—called "prelims" at the end of the first year and "finals" at the end of the last. In the end, work done for the tutor does not count. The finals alone determine the level of the degree—a first, second, and so on—or indeed if there is to be a degree at all.

As a consequence of all this, the lectures at Oxford often have very little to do with the work a particular undergraduate may be doing. Aware of the lecture lists, tutors may assign papers on works that are being presented during the term; but the interests of tutor and student can quickly spin them into areas far distant from the lecturing at St. Cross. For this reason no attendance is taken at lectures, and admittance is routinely given to anyone—such as myself—who requests it of the lecturer. As the only force keeping their rooms from the emptiness of outer space is interest, they often are grateful to anyone expressing it.

After one day in St. Cross Hall, I realized that to have paid the £500 auditor's fee would have been an uncommonly stupid waste of time.

Yesterday I heard one lecture by a Dr. Robbins in a series on the poetry of John Donne, inquiring what religious needs could create such urgency that sexual imagery of great power was required to express it, and conversely what sort of erotic passion would be forced to draw so heavily on religious language. Good stuff to chew over with Jane, I thought, though our major urgency nowadays—surely a spiritual one—seemed remote from the erotic. If a heart was being battered by a three-personed God, it was not Jane's or mine but that of a grieving, pain-filled little boy; and it was his soul we were desperate to see healed.

After the lecture I spoke to Dr. Robbins, who assured me I would be welcome to sit in for the remaining five sessions. The room was not large, with benches for about forty. It had been filled. "Don't worry about the crowd," he said. "Many will be gone after this week."

The second lecture I heard was given by a Professor Carey, on *Dombey and Son*. This is a series on six novels by Dickens. I read a great deal of him in graduate school—including *Dombey*—and each year for the last eight I've taught *Great Expectations* to ninth-graders. Dickens will probably be the last writer I take up this year.

I enjoyed Professor Carey's words. There is something enjoyable about listening to a good lecture, although what it is is hard to define. Ideas are presented and conjoined in various ways, though fluid, always moving toward form, opening wider and embracing more for a time and then contracting and congealing as they approach closure. Part of this fluidity derives from the human voice, with its ephemeral waves lapping upon the porches of our ears, for the lecture exists only in time, not in space. "Wait. What did he say?" we listeners ask ourselves. "What does she mean?" Tension grows from our doubt that such a fluid medium can ever hold a form, although Professor Carey's papers shuffling before him promise that form is there if we can only attend carefully enough to hear it. And when it all does cohere—when Dombey is revealed to us naked and crawling like the bug Dickens with his trickery created him to be—our pleasure is both intellectual and aesthetic. We understand the what and the how, but we also rejoice in the performance that brought us to this understanding.

I am planning to attend one other set of lectures this term: "The Novels of Thomas Hardy," given by a Professor Bayley. I walk into the same room Dr. Robbins used yesterday while the students from the previous lecture are coming out of it. More and more people enter, and I wonder if I should yield my seat to them, whose presence is presumably more legitimate than mine. I slide down the bench to squeeze against the wall, a small, barely noticeable fly on the wall. I zip open my briefcase—here it is, soft and innocent, bereft of all its earlier significance, carrying merely notebooks, pens, a collection of John Donne's poetry.

The room is packed solid when the professor arrives, a small roundish white-haired man with a black gown flapping from his back like bat wings. "I apol-pol-pologize for the si-si-size of the room," he says enthusiastically. "I'll see about getting a bi-bi-bigger one for next week."

John Bayley is a well-known literary critic in England. In reviewing his book *The Characters of Love*, Anthony Powell once characterized Bayley's discussion of Henry James as the grappling of "a pair of oiled and naked wrestlers," a vision that startles all the more when one tries to envision stuffy old James and this ebullient old man going at it in life. Professor Bayley is, I have been told, the husband of Iris Murdoch, who writes wicked, sexy novels of academia—so perhaps the oiled-and-naked-wrestler image is more apt than it first appears.

. For the next forty-five minutes, we are given a series of general observations on Thomas Hardy's work. "Hardy was the mo-mo-most *sensitive* recorder of the second half of the nineteenth cen-cen-century. Much more sensitive than Dickens. More even than Geo-george El-el-el," he pauses and concludes joyfully, "Eliot!"

Hardy, he continues, is heavily influenced by the notion of the cooling universe, of the world running down. At their cores, Dickens and Eliot were more hopeful; Hardy's novels are without much "meliorism." Everything he says fits with the works I am presently reading. He mentions Hardy's reshifting of traditional material in looking forward to modernism, and I see at once what he means when he cites as an example *The Woodlanders*—which I read two weeks ago—a novel in which "living in sylvan beauty becomes a terrifying illustration of survival of the fittest."

Afterward I approach Professor Bayley and ask if I may continue to attend his lectures. When I tell him I am on sabbatical, he fills with immediate energy: "Oh, yes, indee-deed. I'd be honored to have you. Per-perhaps you will have lunch with me some day at my college."

"I'd love to."

I bicycle home through bright sunshine and light breezes.

Yet Wednesday morning dawns after the usual night of tears and lamentation. He woke weeping about midnight, and after a time woke Sam, too; we tried giving him a bath, which sometimes relaxes him; finally he was brought into our bed, and I spent the rest of the night in his. This has become a common occurrence, Jane and I trading off the job of dozing restlessly beside him, while the other spends the night in his bed, alone but asleep.

Around eight o'clock I drive the car to Mr. Young's garage, where it previously was inspected. He too believes it needs a new clutch, and he has one for us. This is a fine car, I know. The Maxi was a gem built to last. But uneasiness fills both Jane and me when we consider putting serious money into it. Still, we agree we don't really have a choice.

While I am gone, Gardner complains of stomachache and refuses to eat, although Jane manages to slip a dose of antibiotics down him. (We have gotten the go-ahead from Dr. Martin.) His reaction is ballistic, but somehow she prevails and the liquid reaches his stomach. I arrive during the settling-down period, and we discuss today's school with him: "This is your field trip, you know. It'll be fun."

"Well, I just don't feel up to it, you know." In the wake of the antibiotic war, he is rational, self-possessed, thoughtful, making the most out of his defeat.

"Everyone is going to Hill End. It's out in the country, a picnic. Mrs. Tattam said she'd like you to come. It will be very relaxed."

"I don't have much energy."

Jane capitulates. "All right. But you and I have to go over to school to tell Mrs. Tattam so she won't wait for you."

"All right."

I know what she's up to. She hopes that the sight of the others about to mount the bus for fun and frolic will inspire him to change his mind. However, he is calm and resolute, pleased (I imagine) that he is getting his way. They walk over together while Sam and I clean up the kitchen. A quarter hour later they are back.

"There you are," she says. "Now I'm going into Oxford today, so you will be staying with Dad and Sam. You can rest, draw, look at books, or play with them. Television only after school time, remember."

"What?" he asks.

"You know that rule," she says neutrally.

"Oh, yeah." He furrows his brow. "I forgot. Wait. I think I'd like to go on the field trip. Is it too late?"

"I don't think so," says his mother with barely concealed pleasure.

In the afternoon, having spent the day partly with Sam awake and partly with *The Older Hardy,* the second half of Hardy's life by Robert Gittings, I walk over to pick up Gardner, leaving Sam still asleep. The bus is pulled up in the school driveway. Most of the children are already off it, buzzing about among parents and each other. I do not see my son.

A teacher I do not know steps off the bus toward me, grim-faced. "He's asleep. I can't seem to wake him. He slept whenever he sat down, I'm afraid. And cried a lot when he had to walk. He seems very weak."

"I'm sorry. I know he is." And I climb onto the bus, take him in my arms, and carry him home, like a sick rabbit or a bird with a broken wing.

Later I read him a letter that came today from his aunt, Jane's sister, a lawyer in New York. He is very fond of her and last Christmas painted a rock for her office to be used as a paperweight. She knows that he is having difficulty here. After expressing concern for his health and spirits, her letter tells that Harrison Ford, the actor, is making a movie in her very own office, and that she left the rock paperweight on her desk so it might appear in the film. It is a charming letter, and my eyes mist as I read it.

Around five o'clock I walk down to Young's Garage and pick up the car. The new clutch costs £135.70.

That night Gardner awakes weeping at nine. We get him back to sleep after a few rubs, but as we sit in the living room I feel my heart a lump of ice in my chest. I remember how pathetic he was on the bus, unable for whatever reason to open his eyes. "He's dying," I say, and I believe myself totally. "He'll die if we keep him here. I know it."

She tries to console me. "No, he won't."

"We are going to have to go home. I know it. To save his life."

"I don't think it's that bad," she says gently. "Let's see what Dr. Moncrief says on Friday."

He awakens again at eleven and is again put back to sleep without difficulty. At two, however, he is crying deeply, desperately. I go in alone to try to comfort him, but he takes no notice of my presence. I take hold of his shoulders, lift him up, and start shaking him. "Gardner!" I snap at him. "Stop! Stop!" His head is waggling like a buoy in a storm, but he continues to weep. "Gardner!"

He opens his eyes and looks at me. "Daddy," he says with sudden and surprising articulation. "Why are you hurting me?"

I cannot answer.

In the next room Sam begins wailing, and Jane comes in beside me. It is a half hour before we can settle both boys, and Gardner and I exchange beds. I cannot forget his astonished expression when he saw who was shaking him so violently.

The next afternoon, Thursday, October 11, I call the Dean of Faculty at my school. I tell him briefly but candidly how things are going—he knows we have been having difficulty, but I doubt he is prepared for this news—and ask if there is any chance we can find a place to stay if we should have to come home. Our house is occupied; an exchange teacher from Spain and his wife are living there for the year we are gone.

"I'll go back to work, if that will make it easier." I am serious. Work seems wildly preferable to what we are doing now.

"Don't worry about that," he says. "Don't worry about anything from here. We can support you somehow. There are a couple of empty apartments. I'm sure we can arrange someplace for you to live. What's important now is that you do whatever you have to so that Gardner gets well."

Afterward, as I hang up the telephone, I cannot tell what is the source of the tears brimming in my eyes, relief or grief, strain or pain, or a mixture too dark and deep for language to color.

17

Yesterday, the day following the field trip, he did not attend school. A wonderful package of letters and pictures arrived in the post from his pals at day care back home; he looked at them vaguely and turned away. Last night came the usual weeping and bed shifting. This morning, Friday, is a day for doctors. After breakfast he and Jane go to the Woodstock Surgery to see Dr. Martin, while Sam and I noodle around the house, washing the dishes, sweeping the kitchen floor. Then we meet them in town where we find the patient licking a popsicle, a.k.a., an ice lolly. We learn that he has been cooperative and cheerful, answering all the doctor's questions and allowing himself to be weighed: 19.3 kilograms, which translates to about forty-three pounds. We think he was close to sixty when we left home. Dr. Martin wants Dr. Moncrief to look at him again, so this afternoon we will be returning to the John Radcliffe, where nothing will be free, although we now understand we will be assisted by Blue Cross/Blue Shield.

Lunch, too, is a cheerful affair, with a good deal of consumption. Jane makes tortellini, and he tucks in two bowls worth. She is buoyed by his attitude.

"Look," she says. "After we see Dr. Moncrief, why don't you drive down to Stoke Poges?"

Stoke Poges is one of the goals I have set for myself. It is the site of the churchyard that Thomas Gray elevated into eternity when he wrote "Elegy Written in a Country Churchyard" in 1751. I studied the poem in college and again last year while preparing for this trip. It is set in the evening as the cows are heading home, and I want to go there to see the churchyard at sunset, to photograph it, and to read the poem aloud.

"Are you sure? I can do it another time."

"Well, let's see how the afternoon goes. But this looks like a good day."

"Knock on wood."

The John Radcliffe trip is without horrors. The boys play happily with the toys and the soft climbing structure in the waiting room. Dr. Moncrief sees us with a minimum of delay. And he sees no pathology.

"Yes, he's thinner, I can see, but I can't see that he's otherwise worse. Whatever he has, it's not progressive, in the sense that it is advancing. In fact, I think he looks quite good at the moment."

I am a trout at a mosquito hatch. How desperately I lunge at these words! The pathetic scarecrow I carried off the bus just two days ago is now a healthy child, albeit a thin one. Dr. Moncrief must be right.

"What are you feeding him now?"

We explain the up-and-down nature of his eating habits. "He takes a cup of apple juice at bedtime," says Jane. "We've tried, but we've never been able to wean him of it. It's a good thing we haven't now, because we've been slipping a liquid vitamin supplement into it. It's a mixture designed for dehydrated patients recovering from flu and other fevers. The chemist suggested it, and I think it helps." She does not mention that he does not know we are doing this. We are certain he will refuse the juice if he discovers it contains any sort of medicine.

Dr. Moncrief looks at us through eyes of calm concern. "Now, as I say, I don't think there's anything in there, a bug, a virus, a blockage. I can run tests if you'd like. A blood test would tell us if it is a virus. I can take some pictures of his tummy, some x-rays. They will cost, but you say your health plan will cover them."

"I think so," I say.

"He is terrified of having blood drawn," says Jane.

"Well, the decision is yours," says Dr. Moncrief. "But I must say, I don't think they're necessary."

I think he is right. I have thought so for a long time, the antibiotics notwithstanding. And I do want very much to believe he is right. "Well then, unless you see a need later on, let's not do any tests that will upset him further."

"Doctor," says Jane, "we think he ought to see a psychological counselor, a child psychiatrist."

Dr. Moncrief makes a tent with his hands. "I think that would make sense."

"When we saw you last, you said you would get us a referral then, so we wouldn't have to wait now if it seemed necessary," she continues.

"I'm sorry. Dr. Forrest was away when I first called, and I've been gone all this week. I'll get in touch with her this afternoon and get you an appointment right away."

"Didn't you say it usually takes a month to get one? I'm afraid we'll be in real trouble if we have to wait that long."

He grows a bit firmer. "I'm sure we can do better than that.

167

She's very good. I'll ask her to fit Gardner in as soon as she can. That's the best we can do."

Driving less than an hour from Oxford southeast on the M40, I come to Stoke Poges, a tiny village about five miles from the edge of the London sprawl. It is nearly four o'clock when I pull onto a side street to ask a passerby how to find the famous churchyard. About a mile or so from the village center I turn in at a sign for St. Giles Church. No spire is visible; at the end of the car park runs only a hedge with a small wooden arched gate leading into what seems a large garden. At first I am unsure where to go. A sign, "GRAY MEMORIAL," points off in one direction, but the words "Remember, this is holy ground," carved in the arch suggest that the church lies beyond it. From the gate I look down a long straight path perhaps a hundred yards long to the church itself.

A wall and second arched gate halfway down the rose-lined path divide the churchyard into two sections. The rose plants are small and well-pruned, bearing large blossoms, yellow, white, pink. The grass is clipped and green, the stones erect, though lichen covers some of them, making them hard to read. Those in the first section date from the late nineteenth century into the twentieth. Those closer to the church are mostly older. Beyond a pasture fence on the right cows are grazing just as they did when Thomas Gray came here some 240 years ago.

Other than the cows, though, it doesn't appear as my mind saw it when I first read the poem. I can remember twenty-five years ago at college visualizing this place: it was misty, for some reason, the grass taller, the stones tilting this way and that. "Country churchyards" in Maine where I grew up are mowed on Memorial Day, Independence Day, and Labor Day; the rest of the time woodchucks tend the lawn. This place is groomed: regular, clipped. It also seemed somehow too new, too straight and narrow. Tall yews and poplars are set at the edges of the churchyard, but the predominant effect is that of open space. I had seen in my mind the gravestones cramped together, shrouded by old twisted trees.

The church is at the western end of the churchyard, where shadows are stretching across the stones. As I approach, I see that this is the oldest section, where the stones do date from the eighteenth century, and the setting begins to approach my imagination. I reflect that probably when Gray was writing, this section constituted the whole churchyard, so I take some photographs here of old stones in dappled and fading sunlight, all the while searching for the poet's grave. I have no idea where to look.

As I stand by the church porch, two couples approach, chatting happily among themselves, clearly out for an afternoon stroll. "Excuse me," I say when they get close enough. "Can you tell me where Thomas Gray is buried?"

"Certainly," says one of the men. "Right around here. This crypt. He's buried with his mother."

It is a large box of gray stone and brick about four feet high, near the east window. The stone carving is worn and lichen-crusted, barely legible; I can make out that Gray's bones are indeed inside next to his mother's. A shy man, never married, he was the only one of twelve children to survive infancy. On top of the vault like a tabletop is a stone that remembers Mrs. Gray as "the careful mother of many children, one of whom alone had the misfortune to outlive her." I photograph the grave even though the dim light gives little hope of success.

"Look right over there," says one of my guides. "See that small window at your feet? That's the 'Leper's Window,' where the village lepers were given alms."

"My God," I say. "When were there lepers in Stoke Poges?"

"I don't know. The Middle Ages, I guess."

"Have you seen the Gray Memorial?" asks one of the women.

"No, not yet."

"Well, it's back through the car park. Don't miss it."

I thank them and head down the long walk, stopping to look back at the church, the sky, the puffing clouds. Following the signs, I come soon to the Memorial: a monstrosity mercifully hidden from both church and churchyard, a huge rectangular construction decorated with quotations from the "Elegy."

I return to the churchyard, taking more photographs in the fading light, when an elderly man who has been working over by the wall opposite Gray's tomb begins to leave. I speak to him: "It's lovely here."

"Yes, it is." He pauses, and then smiles at me. "I was married here."

"Oh?"

"Yes, back in 1939."

"Well, it's lovely."

"It is." He pauses again. "That's her, over there." He points to the flowers he has been setting in.

"Ah. Yes. So it is." We chat comfortably for a few more minutes. After he leaves, I return to the porch where I look over the most ancient stones and begin to read the "Elegy" aloud:

> The curfew tolls the knell of parting day,
>   The lowing herd wind slowly o'er the lea,
> The plowman homeward plods his weary way,
>   And leaves the world to darkness and to me.

My voice is quiet in the gathering dusk, and I am curiously aware of attending to it as if there be two of me, speaker and listener. The poem carries both along with it, enlarging us with its meditations on day and night, fame and obscurity, life and death. I hear again its most famous quatrain:

> Full many a gem of purest ray serene,
> The dark unfathomed caves of ocean bear:
> Full many a glorious flower is born to blush unseen,
> And waste its sweetness on the desert air.

The faint regret in these lines, the mild rue, quivers in my voice. I hear Gardner in them, the dark unfathomed caves, the wasted sweetness. And then, when I least expect it—for honestly I have forgotten that this line is from the poem—Thomas Hardy enters the churchyard: "Far from the madding crowd's ignoble strife." Just two weeks ago I read the story of Gabriel Oakes and Bathsheeba Everdene, but I never expected to find its title here today in Stoke Poges. So, as happened in Winchester Cathedral with Jane Austen and John Keats, two writers previously separate and distinct are conjoined in an unexpected way, leaving me wondering and wiser.

On Sunday Gardner and I are in London visiting my parents. They meet us at Paddington, and he runs to them almost as in the old days, his knees slightly knocking together the way they do. He is happy, all smiles, hugging their legs.

"Did you have a good trip?" my mother asks.

"Yes." He does not hesitate. "Look. I brought my Turtles." He shows her Leonardo and a new Michelangelo, along with the nasty but stupid Rocksteady.

"Oh, good. Let me see." My mother seems always to be able to muster interest in such items.

"I brought some G.I. Joes, too."

171

"Do we walk?" I ask my father.

"Yes. It's only three blocks."

"Great." He can make three blocks, I think. Much farther and I know I will wind up carrying him on my shoulders, no matter how enthusiastic he is now. We stroll toward the door.

"Do you suppose that's where they found Paddington Bear?" my mother asks, pointing at a baggage claim area.

"I don't know," he replies. "Is this where they found Paddington?"

"Oh, yes indeed. Right in this station. That's how he got his name. Look over in the window of that shop. See that great big Paddington?"

"Sam has a little one at home."

The walk is easy, faintly downhill through upscale Bayswater, down Chilworth Street, across Westbourne Terrace—a thoroughfare divided by a mall of trees like Boston's Commonwealth Avenue—and one long block further to Gloucester Terrace and my parents' flat. We enter a marbled hall and climb a flight of dim wide stairs. Gardner has kept up the pace cheerfully, without a sign of discomfort.

Inside we tour the rooms: bedroom in the rear, mirrored and shag-carpeted bathroom, small kitchen with a wide opening like a window to the front room, a tiny bedroom off the front room, all done up in a sort of ecru. French windows open above the street. Gardner is entranced by the balcony and begins setting up his toy soldiers around the balusters. The flat is hugely expensive—£400 a week. My parents were originally planning to share it with my mother's cousin, who fell ill shortly before the trip and had to stay home. Generously she agreed to pay for her share anyway, a lucky break for them, for they would have been severely stretched to foot it all themselves.

"Do you want to use the loo?" asks my mother, grinning with

the word "loo." I remember my grandfather, the old pediatrician, saying "Out the loo," meaning, "Out of the way." I never understood where he came up with the phrase until I heard of the Middle Ages, "Gardey-loo!" having been the cry as the contents of the slop jar were hurled into the street. "Loo," "l'eau," "water": a reasonable etymology.

"What?" asks Gardner.

"The bathroom," she explains.

"No, thank you."

While Gardner plays, we talk around him: their recent trip to the naval museum at Greenwich, a snooker tournament on television, the situation in the Persian Gulf. A couple of weeks ago Saddam Hussein threatened war with Israel; now the news is full of Iraqi nonsense in Kuwait—the tearing apart of oil machinery, the overrunning and looting of businesses, the interning of Kuwaitis, the parading of hostages. My father and I cannot believe there is a peaceful resolution to what is happening, although our perspectives—the war of his twenties was World War II, while my attitudes were shaped by the conflict in Vietnam—are different. Still we both agree Saddam is a bad guy and something is bound to break. Meanwhile, out on the balcony small plastic soldiers continue to wage their own small battles.

"Well, what do you want to do with the day?" asks my mother.

"Honestly, things are so pleasant right now that I think we should just hang out here. Maybe we can try lunch in a bit. God knows if he'll eat anything."

After some paper reading and snooker watching we leave to find an acceptable restaurant. Around the corner on Craven Road we see some expensive ones. Then down a side street we see an Indian tandoori ("No way," I say) and two doors further a sign for hamburgers. "That looks like a good bet."

It is. We all order burgers. My father and I have glasses of good dark beer, while Gardner orders chocolate milk. The burgers arrive nestled juicily in thick buns. Ketchup is available. Gardner eats fully one half of his burger. We all chat comfortably for a time until he starts to squirm. He doesn't want any dessert.

My mother finishes second. "Why don't you two stay here and finish your beers? Gardie and I can go back together."

My father and I settle back with our pints. "He seems in a better mood," he says.

"Yes. I don't know. His energy is so low." I tell him about the field trip on Wednesday. "He hasn't been to school since then. The week after this next one is vacation, and Jane and I are going to keep him at home until after that to see if we can make him stronger. He really can't hack school right now."

Although he doesn't say it, I sense that both he and my mother have a clearer view of the severity of our problem. I do some further explaining anyway. "You know, we haven't had an un-interrupted night's sleep in a month. Every night he wakes up weeping. Almost always one or the other of us has to sleep with him. And what he just ate? The half a hamburger? That was a Thanksgiving dinner."

He murmurs something indicating comprehension, acquiescence, agreement.

"He is acting better today. You're right. But he's so bony. There have been other times we thought he was getting better, but then all of a sudden he gets worse. The best news is we have an appointment for him to see a child psychiatrist."

"Good," he says doubtfully. He has slight faith in doctors of the mind.

"Yes," I say firmly. "It's our last hope, actually."

When we return to the flat, Gardner is coloring in a Teen-age Mutant Hero Turtle coloring book he brought with him. My mother smiles as we enter. "We had a nice walk back," she says. "Someone was vaccinated with a victrola needle."

"Oh?" I say.

"Yes. Very chatty and cheery. Lots of news. I think he's in good shape."

"Wonderful," I say, trying to beat dead the hope that quickens yet again between my rib cage and my heart.

18

*I*t's the following Wednesday, and I'm on the train again to London, this time alone. My mother and I want to visit Kew Gardens. She's an avid horticulturist; at the house in Maine she has several garden plots as well as a number of wildflower habitats for lady's-slippers, trailing arbutus, wild calla, rose pogonia. For me wildflowers are an avocation, occasionally even a vocation, for I have from time to time written articles about them. This year there have been three: a newspaper piece about native orchids from Venezuela (the manuscript recovered in the briefcase), a magazine essay about a Calypso orchid I saw in Vermont, and finally an essay for a scholarly journal on *Impatiens balsamina* in a poem by Emily Dickinson. I understand that Kew Gardens has some of the orchid species I saw in Venezuela.

I'm worried about making this trip. Since Sunday things have grown more unsettled than ever. School is out of the question, for Gardner is too weak to go. On Monday Jane—believing he may have turned the corner—went on a major food shopping trip to the big Tesco supermarket in Kidlington. But he has not eaten well. Furthermore, he still awakens weeping after we are all in bed and insists on moving in with one or the other of us. Last night, after I switched places with him, he wanted our bed to himself, and Jane argued with him angrily, but he was beyond understanding, beyond persuasion. What is left? Love, persuasion, bribery, force: none of these has smoothed England enough to fit him—or, more precisely, smoothed him to fit England—in order that he may be happy.

Instead he keeps growing smaller, shrinking into himself like a dying flower. When I carry him upstairs, my arms might be bearing the bleached bones of a bird, or a sack of dried petals. His limbs are floppy, as if connected by threads, and he often lies bending his legs back so that his feet press mercilessly against his ears. He reminds us of a contortionist we saw in a circus the summer before Sam was born: a tall thin man who unfolded himself from a glass box perhaps two feet square. He could dislocate his joints to wrap his arms and legs more tightly around himself and fill even the corners of the box. We were horrified.

We still have not been able to find out when Gardner may see the psychiatrist. Jane has called Dr. Moncrief twice, but each time he was unavailable and we have not heard back from him. A desperation permeates our lives, bitter and cold, such as I imagine to be the taste and odor of myrrh.

Nevertheless, despite it all we carry on. I went to lectures Monday and yesterday. Although I arrived too late to hear Dr. Robbins on John Donne, Professor Carey startled the undergraduates—shocked a couple, I bet—as he demonstrated that *David Copperfield* is really about women, that in its course all the female characters are in some way or other diminished, and that the only positive relationship in the book is the implicit homosexual one between David and Steersforth. The next day

Professor Bayley finished his overview of Hardy's work and began a chronology, discussing the first novel, *The Poor Man and the Lady*, which was never published and which Hardy destroyed, and most of the second, *Desperate Remedies*, which I just finished last week.

At this lecture I struck up a conversation with another auditor, a young German woman named Agnes. She is working on a doctorate here, a project based on film and theater adaptations of Jane Austen's novels. She did her undergraduate thesis on Hardy and considered focusing the doctoral project on him. After class we discussed the *Wessex Days* production in Chipping Norton, and I described my trip to Stoke Poges.

Then, yesterday afternoon, Jane put on her black shirt and clerical collar to go into Oxford to address the university's Women's Theology Seminar Group. She spoke on being awakened to new possibilities: Barbara Harris's election and consecration as the first woman bishop in the history of the Anglican Communion, Sam's birth on Easter Sunday, her role as priest-in-charge last Advent when the rector retired and the music director died of AIDS. Before the talk a lay Roman Catholic chaplain named Elsie and a few others took her to dinner at an Oxford pub, and afterward Jane Brown, who had attended, drove her home.

"Look," she said and showed me a £10 book coupon from Blackwell's. "They gave me this. I think I'll use it to get the new RSV Bible."

"So it went well?"

"I guess. They were pretty quiet, most of them. One or two seemed a little hostile when they asked questions. But I was glad to get the chance to do it."

When I left this morning, tears were flowing. All the way into London the sky is gray and Gardner's pain nags me. I pick up my mother at the flat on Gloucester Terrace, and we take the Underground to Kew. After a fifteen-minute walk, we find one of the entrances to the gardens, Cumberland Gate.

It is astonishing to see how much is still in bloom in mid-October. The brochure's map shows the layout of the Royal Botanic Garden's three hundred acres: Kew Palace; several conservatories including two huge ones, the Palm House and the Temperate House; two lakes; and everywhere the gathered flora of the world. We amble through a series of plots of aster and potentilla and gentian and lobelia and heaven knows what else. Following the map, we come to the Alpine House.

"Look," I say. "That plant with long gray leaves. I saw it in the Andes in Venezuela. Feel the leaves. Like cotton. It's *frailejon*, the friar plant. Smell it. It's very aromatic."

"Oh, yes," says my mother.

Seeing this plant pleases me. It is another example of the way events in life tie themselves together. Five months ago I was photographing the *frailejon* on Pico Espejo in South America; now I have found it again on the other side of the world. I point out the yellow blossoms: yellow disks with yellow rays, looking like a ragwort or a daisy. "To the people in the Andes these looked like tonsured heads. So they called them after the friars."

We work our way to the Princess of Wales Conservatory, which houses tropical plants, both moist and dry. One room contains a desert habitat with cactus; the next, a huge pool with lily pads large enough—as a photograph proves—to support a baby. Finally we enter the orchid rooms. Not many species are in bloom, but in a corner behind glass I see one—*Epidendrum elongatum*—that I photographed in Merida in June. Did its trip

179

from Venezuela all those years ago (for some of the orchids here are descended from plants that were imported over a century earlier) so confuse its calendar that it can no longer remember when to bloom?

My mother and I have lunch of a sort—dreadful hamburgers —and walk over to the Palm House and around its pond, passing the Temple of Arethusa. I have photographed and written about the wild orchid *Arethusa bulbosa*, named for the goddess of this temple, who turned into a spring trying to escape from Apollo. Then, the gray sky growing darker still, we leave.

My father has gone to a World War II air museum, so we part at Paddington. "We'll see you Saturday afternoon," she says. "I hope things improve."

When I arrive home, Jane is at the end of her tether. Gardner was dreadful during the morning, whining, complaining, weeping, wanting Corn Pops and nothing else. She got angry and shouted at him. After they all took an afternoon trip to the commissary with Lisa, he ate and immediately vomited the bowl of Corn Pops.

At dinner both boys eat something. While they are in the kitchen, Jane and I go into the living room where she breaks into tears. "I don't know," she sobs. "I've been so horrible to him."

"It's O.K.," I say. "It's not your fault."

"It is."

"Look," I say, and decision grows in my voice. "Have we heard from Dr. Moncrief? Does Gardie have an appointment with the psychiatrist yet?"

"No."

"Well, then. Listen. Let's be realistic. We cannot live like this. Let's give them a week. If we don't have an appointment by then, we go home."

She stops crying. "But we can't."

"Sure we can." I don't know if she can hear the relief in me, but I can feel it. Whereas a week ago I swore going home meant ruination, somehow I have moved. Right now it rings with salvation. "The school will help us. It's Gardner. He's got to have help. If they won't give it to us here, we have to go home."

"But—"

"Will you call Dr. Gitlin? Tell her what's going on? Alert her that we might be coming back and what we'll need. I'll call the school again just to keep them in the picture."

"Are you sure?"

I let something go, what I'm not sure. "One week. At the latest. We can't live like this."

On Thursday Jane goes over to the Woodstock Primary School to a meeting requested by Mrs. Tattam. It turns out to be official, the school presenting a position that Gardner is not well enough, physically or emotionally, to attend.

"They offered to help," she tells me upon her return. "They said that sometimes they can pressure the system to move more quickly. They can put some pressure on Dr. Moncrief. But the fact remains, they're cutting us loose."

"Oh, shit." Neither of us speaks. Finally I say, "Maybe we should ask them to help in getting the appointment."

"If it doesn't happen soon, I'll ask them to get involved."

But as it happens, the school's assistance is not required. Later that afternoon, at 3:45, we speak with the secretary for Dr. Gillian Forrest at the Park Hospital for Children, who gives Gardner an appointment for Tuesday, October 23, at 10:00 A.M. Once again, hope—which Emily Dickinson once described as "the thing with feathers"—flutters within us.

181

As if in a sort of celebration, Jane brings out a present she bought Gardner earlier this month and has until now put away: a video of a movie he loved back home, *E.T.* He is excited, speaking in a voice we sometimes hear at such times, the Good Baby. "Ooo, ooo. Me like *E.T.* Me want to watch it."

He and I sit watching, my arm over his shoulder, his head against my chest, his thumb in his mouth. The little boy in the film, Elliot, discovers a little lost alien and brings it home despite the teasing of the other children. My son laughs as Elliot, fully empathetic with E.T., becomes drunk at school when the alien begins drinking beer from the refrigerator at home. Before, whenever we watched this film, I always saw Gardner identify with Elliot, the outsider, who perseveres against the establishment— the teachers, the scientists, the police, the adults—and, cycling across the sky, sets E.T. free.

Now the film reaches the moment when the extraterrestrial seems to be dying, its gray skin turned white beneath the sterile lights of the operating theater. I look down at Gardner, pale, thin, wasting away. "E.T., phone home," he says, and again, "E.T., phone home," pain suffusing his face, and I know with a twist of terror that he is watching his own life wind down before his own eyes, and, worse, that he understands what he is watching as he says once more, pale and hopeless, "E.T., phone home."

On Friday afternoon I go into his room. He is lying on his bed, gazing into space. "How are you feeling?"

He turns toward me lethargically, not recognizing me it seems, and then focuses. "Oh, Dad."

"Yes."

"Here." He holds his hand out slowly. His other hand is at his mouth, making it difficult to understand the words slithering past his thumb. "This is for Peter." With a shock I see that he is giving away Leonardo, the Teenage Mutant Hero Turtle.

It is ten o'clock on Saturday night. My parents are here, having arrived late in the afternoon from visiting some friends of theirs who drove them up to Woodstock from some town just north of London. Dinner was served in two shifts. The boys began with Kraft macaroni and cheese, but Gardner wouldn't touch it and so ate a few Corn Pops. Then we put them to bed. The adults had a big dinner of ham, broccoli, potatoes, apple crisp, bread, wine; but there was little joy in it.

Some of the sadness on our side stemmed from a rather petty regret, one we do not express. At one time we had hoped to use the grandparents as babysitters so we could go out together to dinner, to the fancy Bear Hotel, say. Since we arrived in England, we have left the boys at home with a sitter only one time, and that was to go across the street for that evening with the Browns. But now we don't dare leave them alone, for fear Gardner might erupt. So this good-bye dinner for my mother and father signaled the end of a specific hope—and of a more general one, too, that they might somehow imbue our withering child with desire to eat, to smile, to flourish.

We didn't really talk much about it during dinner. After all of the stops and starts of hope that this year will come around right, I seem to have come to the end of caring. What will happen, will happen. *Qué será, será,* as Doris Day put it so many years ago when I was not much older than Gardner. A chilly mist of pain wraps us all, even Sam, who woke in tears last night, unprompted by his brother.

While we are eating, we hear him start to scream. Not weep,

---

scream: long high cries of pain, as though he is being beaten: "Mommy! Mommy! Eeee!"

Jane goes up to quiet him, while my parents and I stumble through a conversation. Then I excuse myself and go up to help. They are in our room on the bed, and she is cradling him in her arms. I come and rub his legs, which are rigid with cramps. "Oh! Oh! Oh!"

After a time I return downstairs. "He's settling down, I think." The screams have quieted but Jane does not reappear. Finally, we decide to call it a night.

As we climb the stairs, crying still comes from our room. Pausing in the hall, my mother says, "Can I help?"

"No, it's O.K.," I say, my stomach frozen. "You go up and try to get to sleep. He'll be all right in a bit." I go in.

"Daddy," he sobs. "Daddy."

I take Jane's place, massaging his feet and calves, rubbing his bony feet. "There, there," I say.

"Would you like to hear a story?" Jane asks.

The sobs start to slide into soft gasps, but he does not reply.

"How about *St. George?*"

"O.K." I can hardly hear him.

And she begins to read, gently and softly, about the Red Cross Knight, who, accompanied by Princess Una and her dwarf, gazes up at the Celestial City before passing on to battle the savaging dragon. I leave our bedroom—in which we have not spent a full night together in more than two weeks—and get into his bed. Soon she comes in, and we hold each other in the dark for a while in terror. Then she goes back to him.

Perhaps we do sleep. However, at 12:30 he is screaming again, and I rush in to them. These are the same high shrieks of pain and despair, and they will not stop. He is lying on the floor wedged against the far side of the bed and the wall, his body contorted, his legs twisting as he pulls them behind his head. We hug him, kiss him, shout at him, shake him: he will not stop screaming. His muscles are knotted and thrumming in agony. I lift him into the middle of the bed, where we try to envelop him on both sides. The screaming continues, unabated.

Time, the most elastic of dimensions, unhinges; we three are in a black hole of screaming that seems without beginning or end. In a burst of objectivity, like an underwater swimmer bursting for air, I emerge momentarily to wonder where my parents are, if they hear this, but they do not appear, thank God, for what can they do? Then I am again engulfed in the screams. Somehow he is back on the floor. At last I look at my watch, which at least may be presumed to be unaffected by what is happening: 1:10. He has been screaming for more than half an hour. "Jane," I say. "Can you hold on?" I might as well be talking to her in the middle of a cyclone. "I'm going to call the hospital."

She nods.

"What's the hospital's name? Where our appointment is?"

"The Park. Children's Hospital. It's Dr. Forrest."

Downstairs I tremble as I turn the TelCom book. What will I say? We have no relationship with this hospital yet. We know no doctor there. I find the number and dial. It rings and rings, and above me I hear my son's screaming.

Finally, a voice. "Allo? Hospitals." The accent is foreign, Indian perhaps.

"Is this the Park Hospital?"

"Yass."

"I'm dealing with an emergency. Can I speak to someone who can help?"

"One moment."

Again the sound of ringing and ringing. I fear it will never end. But at last another voice, a woman, kindly tones: "Hello."

I begin talking fast, the words tumbling out. "Hello. I'm calling from Woodstock. My son is having an emotional crisis. We have an appointment for him at the Park with Dr. Forrest. I know she's not there, but he's weeping violently and we can't seem to stop him. Can I get him admitted if I drive over there now?"

The soft voice replies, "I'm sorry. I wish I could help. I'm afraid you've been connected to the wrong hospital."

"What?"

"We share the same answering service with the Park at night and on the weekends. If you ring this number again, I'm sure they will get you over there."

"Thank you." I hang up, numb with fear. We *are* alone here, completely. We have no one to call for help, no place to turn to. I want to weep, but lack the strength, lack even the strength to press the buttons on the telephone. It is as if I have been injected with embalming fluid. I can only listen. Upstairs all is quiet.

So I can move, after all. When I get up to the bedroom, I find Jane patting a small boy curled into a fetal position holding a blanket and sucking his thumb.

"He's better, now," she says. "He doesn't want to go to the hospital. He would like you to sleep with him."

"I'd like that." I tell her briefly about the hospital call, then slide in beside him. She turns out the light and leaves us alone in the dark.

I can't analyze anything. My mind whirls so fast it grows dark as the room, and I concentrate only on breathing, slow and deep and regular, willing similar slow and deep and regular respiration upon my son, who lies beside me rigid, iron-stiff. We are both silent as I stroke him gently and kiss his cheek. He does not move but holds his position like a statue. In my caresses I am tentative, for I have no wish to unleash those cries again. We must make it to the dawn.

As before, time unhinges, seconds becoming hours and vice versa. I have no idea how long we lie there in the dark together—his rigidity rocklike and unyielding—until faintly I hear him begin to moan.

"Do you want to watch a movie?" I ask.

"Which one?" he asks faintly, as though through thick fog.

"I have a science fiction one you've never seen." A few nights ago I taped David Lynch's *Dune* from a late-night broadcast. I have seen it before: dark, nightmarish, but surely preferable to what I have been watching up to now.

"Okay."

By my watch it is nearly three o'clock as we come down the stairs. I lay him on the couch and cover him with a blanket, then start the film, returning to take his head on my lap. For nearly three hours, as the night eventually becomes the day, *Dune* unrolls before us, with the weird creatures of the desert planet Arrakis: the Fremen sand-dwellers with their totally blue eyes, Paul Muad'dib and his prescience, the horrible Baron, the terrible sandworms fifty meters long or more. Before the film is quite over, sometime after five, he falls at last to sleep, and I am alone with my weary head. I do not turn off the tape, however, until the credits are rolling. Then I too take some sort of rest.

When Jane comes downstairs around six-thirty, she finds us there. I am awake to greet her. "We can't stay here any more," I say. "We have to leave."

"You think so?" her face drawn with pain.

"We can't stay." We hug. "We have to go home."

19

*T*wo hours later, further decisions have been made. Jane has called the twenty-four-hour British Air number and booked seats for her and the boys to Boston for Tuesday morning. The price is something more than £600. She has managed to get on the same plane my parents will be on, figuring that, if either boy should have a problem on the flight, she can enlist a grandparent's assistance. I will stay on in England for another week or ten days to close up our affairs: sell the car, pack the rest of our things, clean Hereford House. Also I can take a tour of Dorset and thus finish my Hardy project. Three of his novels remain to be read: two unknowns, *The Hand of Ethelberta* and *The Trumpet-Major,* and one studied in college, *Jude the Obscure.* I actually picked up *Jude* a week or so ago, but remembering how depressing it is—especially with the deaths of Jude's children—I couldn't face it. I wonder if I will be able to any time soon.

Ambivalence fills Jane like water in a glass: visible, brimming. Some part of her still hopes we can stay. "I just don't think we've exhausted every opportunity," she says. "His appointment with Dr. Forrest is the day we leave. We don't know if she can do anything."

"It's too late. He's inches from the hospital. We can't let him slide any more."

"You think going home will prevent that?"

From somewhere I fill my voice with confidence. "I do."

"Do you remember what you said before? We were outside, with Sam on the fence watching goggies. You said it would take a hell of a lot of therapy to forgive him if he made us go home. Remember?"

I do. And with a start I realize that I have moved an ocean's distance from that anger. I know he has not done this to us deliberately. No one would inflict such pain on himself out of choice. He is not making us go home, I understand. We are choosing to do so; I am choosing to do so. And I realize that the emotion suffusing me is not pain, or anger, or even fear. It is pure blessed relief.

When Gardner wakes up about eight o'clock, we explain our decision to him. "Sweetie," says Jane, stroking his head on the couch, "we have decided to go back home. It just isn't fair to have you being this unhappy."

He looks into her eyes blankly, puts his thumb in his mouth, and rolls over to face the back of the couch.

Somewhat later my mother and father come downstairs. Gardner is in front of the television and

Jane and Sam are cooking breakfast. I meet my parents on the stairs. "Did you sleep O.K.?"

"Yes," says my mother. "We didn't hear anything. What about you?"

Dismay covers their faces as they listen to the events of the night. "Jane got tickets on your flight. We decided to go home."

"You don't have any choice," they tell me.

Jane takes my parents into Oxford to the train station and then goes to sing Eucharist at Christ Church. She has wanted to do this since we arrived. Dazed with lack of sleep, I stay home and watch Sam noodle and Gardner doze.

In the afternoon I call the Walters, our colleagues from whom we are renting Hereford House. They are sorry, sympathetic, supportive, also prepared for our decision. In fact they have been doing some telephoning for us. "We have some good news," they say. "It looks like you will be able to get your house back." The couple from Spain, having been apprised of Gardner's situation, has volunteered to move into a school-owned apartment. We should call the Dean of Faculty to confirm this. When I do so, he tells me not to worry, that our house will be available for us. I am nearly weeping when I hang up.

Jane calls a parishioner from her former church, a woman who has been aware of and extremely sympathetic to our plight all along. She invites us to stay at her house until we can move back into our own. "They have lots of room," she tells me. "And a swimming pool. Maybe Gardner will like it. Remember how enthusiastic he was about the town pool." Then her face stiffens in pain.

Jane and Martyn Brown come over for Sunday evening dinner: chicken, rice, broccoli, salad, French bread, and pear crisp. They give good medicine, dispensing kindness and humor in large doses. The evening passes too quickly.

On Monday I take Sam for a morning walk through Blenheim while Jane packs. It is a lovely morning of rising mists, cool at first but warming with the sun. When we return, there are piles of clothes and things everywhere and Jane is overflowing with sadness and frustration.

"It's all wrong. We're making the wrong decision. We shouldn't have given in to him."

We are in the garden, talking where he will not hear us. I put my arm around her shoulders and turn her toward the French windows, beyond which on the couch he is lying. "Go in and look at him, Jane. Look at him. We don't have a decision to make. Not any more. It's O.K." Somehow I comfort her, by saying things which mostly I believe are true.

At noon I am listening to Professor Carey lecture about *Bleak House*, a novel that wore me to the ground when I read it in college and did so a second time when I watched it a couple of years ago on PBS. The lecture itself seems very technical and academic, concerned with Dickens's inability to deal with his material—the stories of Lady Dedlock's irregular love affair and of the Chancery Court's bewildering morass—and the consequent displacement of those two narratives. What I remember about the book is more concrete: the pain of Esther Summerson, the spontaneous combustion of the evil Krook, the broken lives hanging about the Chancery Court. I return to my own bleak house.

The two Janes are sitting in the kitchen. The air is thick with distress, to which Jane Brown is applying comfort, tea, and a lardie cake—a big sticky bun. My wife has just telephoned her mother, who reacted to the news of our capitulation somewhat as my father did on my parents' first night in Woodstock, although more emphatically: Gardner is manipulating us, we should stick it out, we are making a serious mistake both for him and ourselves. My Jane—unfortunately far too vulnerable to withstand such advice—was still weeping bitterly when Jane Brown arrived. I find myself filled with anger, not so much because of her mother's words, but because of their effect.

Gardner comes into the room as we talk. Jane Brown looks up at him. "He does have that Belsen look about him, doesn't he?"

"What's that?" I ask.

"Belsen?" she says. "Like Auschwitz or Dachau?"

"Oh, right. The concentration camp," says Jane. "For some reason we don't talk so much about Belsen in the States. Yes, he does, doesn't he?" And somehow she manages a smile.

Jane and Sam stop by the surgery to give the news of our departure to Dr. Martin. It is late, nearly seven, when she returns. "I had to wait a long time, but he was very nice," she tells me. "Said he felt they hadn't done enough for us. No kidding. At first he wanted us to give the system another chance. Said he would get Gardie admitted to the hospital for tests. But I told him we were committed to going home. He asked me if we had considered that it was psychological." She snorts. "But he did raise an interesting possibility. The boys and I can go home, and if the doctors think we can turn him around by Christmas, say, maybe we can come back."

This sounds reasonable, and it will give us a positive focus for the glum prospect of returning to the States. What the hell. "Sure. They'll have some idea of his prognosis. It might work."

The flight leaves Heathrow's Terminal Four at 10:00 A.M. My family must be there two hours before departure. With the morning traffic we must leave at least an hour and a half before that. In consequence we need to get up around 5:00.

With the boys in bed she continues to pack while I head off to the tandoori restaurant for take-out. On the wall is a mural of a river scene, in the foreground a sloe-eyed woman in a sari, who looks at me compassionately as I wait for the order. Upon my return Jane is discovered moving glassily through our bedroom and the upstairs hall from pile of stuff to pile of stuff.

"Come and eat," I tell her. She is exhausted, drained of energy and spirit.

After the prawns and *nan* we return to the packing. She has been organizing things into the immediately accessible, the necessary, the useful, and the not needed until later. I begin jamming things into two suitcases and a duffel bag. The rest I shall carry later. How will she manage the two boys and three huge bags? I wonder. It is after midnight when we go to bed.

At 3:00 in the morning both boys are up and weeping. Jane goes in with Sam, I take Gardner.

We are up at 5:15 and ready to go by 6:00. Neither of us has had more than three hours of sleep. It is still dark. As we load the boys into the car, Jane Brown comes across the street to give my family good-bye hugs and kisses. She is crying.

At 8:10 we arrive at the airport. I drop them off at the unloading area and park the car. When I finally find them among the crowds at Terminal Four, they are checked in and ready to enter the departure lounge. "Did you see my parents?"

"No. But they've checked in. I asked. They've probably already gone through security."

"Good. You can find them if you need them."

She nods.

"Call me," I say. "I'll be back from Dorset sometime Friday." I hold her tight, then rewrap them all in my arms, my two sons and wife, my pretty chickens and their dam, my fragile family bound for home.

In his lecture Professor Bayley is talking about Hardy's second novel *Under the Greenwood Tree:* "Hardy wrote this no-no-novel as a deliberate exercise in the rustic pastoral." An acceptable characterization: when I read it a month ago, I wrote in my journal that it was "simple," that it allowed Hardy to "settle into the landscape and the people."

The novel tells of the Dewey family, Reuben and his son Dick, who are members of the "Mellstock quire," musicians at the local church. It draws on Hardy's own church playing in his youth. Rural music, secular and sacred, runs through the book; the title in fact comes from a broadside ballad about country folk disporting themselves "under the greenwood tree." In the plot, such as it is, the "quire" is to be supplanted by a lovely young organist named Fancy Day, with whom Dick Dewey predictably falls in love.

"Fa-Fa-Fancy Day is one of the very few failures among Hardy's heroines," says Professor Bayley. He's right. Utterly idealized through Dick's eyes, possessing neither mind nor matter, she evaporates next to Bathsheba Everdene or Tess Durbeyfield or Eustacia Vye.

It helps my spirits to listen and take notes, but when the lecture ends, my stomach sinks again. Agnes, the German student, has been sitting next to me again today, and I have told her about my family's departure this morning. Afterward we walk to the Junior Common Room—a sort of snack bar—for coffee and a sandwich.

"So tomorrow I'm going to Dorset for a couple of days, to look for vestiges of Hardy. Then it's clean the house, sell the car, and fly home. Unless there's a miracle, and he can come back."

"That's dreadful." Her voice is soft with a slight accent, her eyes brown, sympathetic. She is a nice person, somewhere in her twenties, in Oxford for a year.

195

"In a way this little trip to Hardy country makes it sort of bearable. I'll finish work on him. At least I get a sense of closure. It's harder for my wife. She's just gotten her things moving, and now she has to go home, with nothing finished."

We talk about Agnes's work. She mentions some plays in the area: a modern-dress version of Jane Austen's *Emma* in Chipping Norton, a treatment of Hardy's *Tess* in Coventry. I tell her I'd like to see the latter. "If you decide to go after I get back from Dorset—Monday would be best, because my wife is calling sometime this weekend—maybe we can do it together. If the doctor says the boy shouldn't return, I'll be going home Wednesday or Thursday."

"The play would be nice." She seems pleased.

I give her my phone number. "Call on the weekend. I'll be around most of the time, cleaning."

Late Wednesday morning all the elements of the Stonehenge monument—three huge sarsen trilithons, uprights and lintels of what remains standing of the sarsen circle and the smaller stones, and those that have fallen—stream with rainwater, as has happened so often during the last 3,500 years. Poncho-covered, I stream with them, given respite only when I pay the admission fee and walk through the tunnel under the road. A chain boundary holds tourists back from the great stones so they must be circled at a distance of twenty or thirty feet. Still, the tallest sarsen stone being twenty-two feet high, one is moved in their presence.

Eight years ago Jane and I came here on our honeymoon. While bicycling around England, we stopped in Salisbury for a night. The next day we took a bus to Amesbury and walked the two miles north of town to the monument. After we crossed the A303, we stood looking down a long grassy decline to the circle, still a half mile away, yet already immense. "My God," I said. "Can you imagine the first Romans marching over the hill and looking down at that? 'Jumping Jove, Claudius! Who the Styx put those things up? Giants! Let's get our butts back to Rome, *celeter!*'"

I have returned to the henge today out of respect for *Tess of the D'Urbervilles,* for Stonehenge is where Tess and Angel Clare are captured, having spent the night among the great stones and the winds, which together create a strange music in the dark: "a booming tune, like the note of some gigantic one-stringed harp." The place is an apotheosis of timelessness, where Tess and all her sorrows, watched over by her weak and puny Angel, lay suspended for a night within the ancient forest of stones. I stand for a time imagining what it would be like to be a fugitive and sleep the night here. Then I try to photograph the stones without including signs or restraining chains or other tourists.

A few miles beyond Stonehenge, I stop at a BP station. A woman is pumping the petrol, and we start chatting.

"You like Hardy? Good for you," she says. "I go to a discussion group monthly and we just finished *Return of the Native.* I had never read it before."

How many gas station attendants in America would speak to me like this? I try to hide my astonishment, but not my enthusiasm. "Really? I always had a thing for Eustacia Vye. What a woman! But when I read it this time, I had to admit she was a handful. A bit spoiled."

"Well, she didn't have it so easy, did she?" She smiles and gives me my change. "Have a lovely trip."

The next morning I am up bright and early. Yesterday afternoon the Dorchester Tourist Information Centre sold me a series of pamphlets, each a tour for a specific

Hardy novel, and then sent me to stay at the bed-and-breakfast of a Mrs. Broadway for £15 a night. I found her kind, the room comfortable and new. After establishing myself *chez* Broadway, I explored my way to Hardy's birthplace in Higher Bockhampton, about three miles from town. This tiny hamlet, together with the equally tiny Lower Bockhampton and Stinsford, became Mellstock in the novels' geography. This house was Reuben Dewey's in *Under the Greenwood Tree:* "a long low cottage with a hipped roof of thatch." The sky was still mostly cloudy and the house open only "By Appointment," so I looked a while and resolved to return the next day when the sun might be shining. And so today it is.

Later last evening I walked about town looking for a place to eat, finally settling on *The Country Gentleman,* mostly because of its sign offering "Hardy Meals and Wessex Ales." The folks inside were friendly and cheerful. I asked about the ale.

"Wessex Ale? It's been around for a long time."

"Oh. I thought it might be named after Hardy's book of short stories. Called *Wessex Tales.*"

"Naow. Don't think so. It's quite good, usually. Don't drink any now, though. This last barrel we got's a bad'un."

This morning after Mrs. Broadway's hardy breakfast of cereal, fried egg, toast, fried tomato, bacon and banger, I set off to explore Dorchester. The Barclay's where I withdraw money from the automatic teller machine is a brick building; to the left of the door hangs a round blue plaque, similar to the one in Lyme Regis on the house Jane Austen lived in: "This house is reputed to have been lived in by The Mayor of Casterbridge in Thomas Hardy's story of that name written in 1885."

The morning is bright and breezy, white clouds scudding about the sky. With the pamphlet "The Country of *The Mayor of Casterbridge*" by Norman J. Atkins in hand, I begin at the top of the town at the statue of Hardy, eternally avuncular seated on a granite base, and walk down High Street past the Corn Exchange, the site of Michael Henchard's—Hardy's doomed Mayor—rise and fall. Just beyond is the King's Arms Hotel, with its first-floor bow-window jutting over the street, where Henchard's long-lost wife Susan, standing in the street below, first saw him as mayor holding forth at a public dinner. At the base of the hill the road crosses first one and then another branch of the River Frome. At the second bridge—from which melancholy residents of Casterbridge used to gaze into the water and ruminate—I take a path to "Ten Hatches," the weir where Henchard considered committing suicide.

A weir is a dam with a series of hatches that can be raised or lowered for flood control. In the book, while Henchard stood here, an effigy dressed in his clothes—used earlier by some of the baser Casterbridge residents to lampoon him—came floating by. The sight of himself apparently drowned restored him to his senses. I look hard into the river, but nothing is here but limpid water and grasses.

Still, it is powerful, how much of Hardy's work remains. Returning to Mrs. Broadway's house and my car, I drive south in the town to the Maumbry Rings, a Roman amphitheater built on the site of a neolithic henge. Susan and Henchard met here to discuss their plans of remarriage. Then I stop for a moment at the high brick walls of Max Gate, the house Hardy built for himself—"No Visitors" reads a sign, and a second, "Watch Out for Cats"—before I find my way out to Maiden Castle.

Hardy called this place "Mai-Dun, of huge dimensions and many ramparts." It is a great prehistoric earth-fort, a mile southwest of the edge of town, rising from flat green fields to a height of perhaps eighty feet. As I pull into the car park at the base, an army of dark clouds comes rolling across the sky. I put on my plastic poncho and begin walking up a steep path through grassy ramparts. At the top, the scale is tremendous: a flat expanse nearly a half mile long and two hundred yards wide rimmed by a three-foot berm. When Stonehenge was under construction, another group of people were building this place as the site for a fortified town. My pamphlet tells me that Michael Henchard came here "glass in hand" to spy on his daughter Elizabeth-Jane walking with Donald Farfrae on the Budmouth Road.

The rain, accompanied by a strong wind, whips my poncho about me. Three children in yellow slickers and blue wellies are dashing about, reduced to tiny specks of color by the vast plain. How can I avoid thinking of Gardner and Sam, who should be here? Then a swathe of sun splashes through, across the top of Maiden Castle and onto the fields below; specks of cow gleam black and bright white in the distance, and a rainbow arcs over them and Dorchester beyond. It is a promise.

In the afternoon the sunshine is back and I return to Higher Bockhampton. Luckily, for I have made no appointment, Hardy's birthplace is open. For £1.70 I can wander through the rooms of his early life, and those of Dick Dewey's too, running fingers over his dining room table, stopping at the upstairs window seat where he wrote his first poems. Out the back door lies the Egdon Heath of *Return of the Native*, really a combination of Blackthorne and Puddletown Heaths. It is forested these days, but the floristic markers of heathland remain: bracken fern, gorse or furze, and heather. Walking along paths, I come at last to a hill called "Rainbarrow," from which Eustacia Vye stood looking toward *The Quiet Woman Inn* (the logo of which was a headless woman) and Damon Wildeve. I gaze, too, but it is daytime and no light shines from that direction anymore—if it ever did.

Returning to the car, I follow the map in "The Country of *The Return of the Native*" by J. P. Skilling to a dirt road. This is my last stop on the Eustacia Vye trail. The walk in takes about ten minutes, past woods and fields alive with pheasant. They scuttle through the bushes and bask in the sunshine, breaking into flight at my approach, scores of animated, iridescent rainbows. Then a gate in a fence opens to the river. At this spot concrete embankments and brown sheets of steel comprise the weir that Hardy named Shadwell. Here, despite the efforts of Diggory Venn, Wildeve and Eustacia drowned.

From the bank I pick up a piece of broken flint, a hemisphere worn and white on the outer crust, fresh and gray at the core, and put it in my pocket. The Frome flows quietly this time of year. It bears little resemblance to the whirlpool at the climax of *Native*, but I fill it full and rushing in my mind, listening for faint echoes of the shouts of the drowning lovers, and of Clym Yeobright, who was saved.

I have one more place to visit in Hardy's world: St. Michael's Church, Stinsford. Lying halfway between Higher Bockhampton and Dorchester, here is where the "Mellstock quire" played. Here too is where Hardy wished to be buried. The *Blue Guide to Literary Britain* says that he once called this place his Stoke Poges. Stinsford is today smaller and homelier than Gray's village ever was, but it surely has received as much elegizing as Stoke Poges.

Even from the car park I can see the church's architecture rising with each successive section: chancel, nave, and a short square tower. A flag path leads around to the west entrance. The Hardy family graves are set just beside this path, clearly marked. Unlike those of Gray, the gentle bachelor lying dustily with his "careful mother," Hardy's remains have been somewhat more violently distributed. I stand before a coffin-sized marble tomb lying above ground, and in the inscriptions around three sides the bizarre story of his burial is evidenced.

His first wife, Emma Gifford, died in 1912. She had been a giddy, attractive woman when they married, but in subsequent years she grew heavy and grumbling, and Hardy simply ignored her. During the last two days of her final and painful illness he did not go upstairs to see her until five minutes before she died. He was left—quite deservedly—prostrate with guilt and grief. He wrote dozens of poems to her memory, he who hadn't written one about her for more than a decade. Two years later at the age of seventy-four he recovered enough to marry thirty-five-year-old Florence Dugdale. Still the guilt remained.

When Hardy died at last in 1928, his aggressive literary advisor, Sidney Cockerell, arranged for him to be buried in Westminster Abbey. Florence protested mightily, reminding everyone that he had always asked to be buried with Emma. A compromise was reached: his heart was removed from the corpse and put into the tomb, while the rest of him was shipped to London. When Florence died in 1937, she was buried with Emma and whatever remained of the heart. On one side of the tomb, then, is engraved Emma's name; on the other, Florence's; and on the front:

HERE LIES THE HEART OF
THOMAS HARDY, O.M.
SON OF THOMAS AND JEMIMA HARDY

Inside the church is a brass plaque to Hardy's father and the other members of the quire set there by Hardy and his brothers and sisters. A handsome rank of organ pipes, together with the instrument itself, was donated by Katherine Hardy, the novelist's sister. I sit a while in the church, gazing at sunlight playing through the windows across the organ and the mahogany pews, trying to see Hardy, boy and man, moving through this space. At last I leave. It is late. Tonight I have a dinner reservation in *The King's Arms*, where once Michael Henchard ate, and surely Thomas Hardy, too. I am nearly finished here.

20

_____

I arrive home from Dorset late in the afternoon. Hereford House is as empty and still as the Stinsford churchyard. Leaving the car on the street, I carry stuff— books, suitcase, camera equipment—inside in two trips and lay out the notes and pamphlets from the journey. Then I turn on the television for the news.

Four days ago—the date of my family's departure—former Prime Minister Edward Heath brought thirty-three British hostages back from the clutches of Saddam. The BBC is still showing features of release, of homecoming, of joyful reunion. What is happening with my own repatriated hostage? I ask myself, watching a procession of joyful faces flicker over the screen.

After a supper of leftovers I sit reading *The Hand of Ethelberta*, Hardy's only attempt to write like Jane Austen. Ethelberta Chickerel (where *did* he get those names?), a butler's daughter, has married upstairs, so to speak, and has been richly widowed, all before she is twenty. Now she lives with her wealthy mother-

_____

in-law, chatting wittily in sitting rooms while the rest of her family works in service below. Crossing class lines seems to have obsessed Hardy, but his characters are most comfortable on the lower levels. The higher they rise, the cruder and less believable they turn. In this he's the opposite of Jane Austen, whose lowest-class people are more refined and better behaved than any of Wessex's gentry.

Around nine o'clock the phone rings. It's Jane. The connection is as clear as if she is at the Browns across the street.

"Hey. How are you all?"

"We're fine." I release my breath. "I'm calling from the Walters."

"How's Gardie?"

"Tired. Weak. But he's very glad to be back home. When we got into the lounge at Logan, he hugged me and said, 'Thank you, Mommy.' "

It turns out that she has already seen a family counselor— a clinical social worker—and Gardner has an appointment with him on Monday. The counselor was recommended by Dr. Gitlin, the pediatrician, who has supported the decision to bring him home in the strongest terms. His weight is forty-one pounds, a loss of thirteen from his last physical examination way back in January, more accurately nineteen or twenty from when we arrived. He is significantly dehydrated, his electrolyte count way out of whack. Otherwise there is no indication of physiological pathology.

"So," I ask finally, "do you think I should get tickets home? Or do you think he'll be well enough to come back before Christmas?"

"I asked Dr. Gitlin. She said, 'You can if you want. But why take the risk?' I got the point. Better buy your tickets."

After the call I have no strength to read and so watch television for a while. But nothing is on, Hereford House is chilly. About ten o'clock I crawl into bed to sleep.

Now in the morning I am standing with my jaw tight, looking over the fence at nothing, at an empty space. "Fuck," I remark. Someone has stolen the car.

It's my own damn fault; I forgot to go out that last time to park it and bring in the keys. I was too tired. Shit. I gape for a minute up and down the empty street, then go inside to call the police station. A voice gives me a number, telling me to inform the Thames Valley Police central office. All car theft in Oxfordshire has been centralized, perhaps the better to deal with what America calls the chop-shop industry. With luck Inspector Morse will get the case. An officer at the Kidlington station takes all the information about the poor old Maxi and tells me they will let me know if anyone finds it.

"I can't believe anyone thought it was worth any money," I tell him.

"Perhaps not. It may turn up." His voice registers all the optimism of a trainer of old dogs.

Paul White is in many ways a mirror-image of what I have until recently been: a New England preparatory teacher on sabbatical living in Woodstock with his wife and two sons. A math teacher, he did two years of postgraduate work at Oxford, and so has brought his family to spend his year amid surroundings which, for him at least, are familiar. The eastern U.S. prep-school community is not large, and Paul and I have a number of common acquaintances, but for some reason we have seen little of each other during the fall. His boys are young, but neither is in Gardner's class. He and I chatted briefly at the school fair and agreed we should go out sometime to a pub.

A box of American food is balanced on my bicycle's handlebars. Corn Pops, Oscar Mayer wieners, Jello, Kraft macaroni and cheese: these delicacies mean nothing to most residents of Woodstock—except the Whites. This box may even help them avoid a crisis like ours, although their boys seem to have adjusted well. A part of me is envious of this fact. Just as I push open the Hereford House gate, one of the local police constables is driving by. I wave him over.

"Did they tell you about my car?" I ask.

"No. What's the trouble?" He is friendly, concerned; I don't know his name, but I've seen him before.

It seems silly of the Thames Valley Police central auto theft bureau not to involve the local constables. Surely this is a goddamn Woodstock yobbo, some kid who took it out for a joyride and has left it somewhere in a ditch. Who in the world would steal that car for profit? Even knowing of its new clutch?

"I'll have a look around town. It may turn up."

"Thank you."

Two hours later Paul and I are walking back to Hereford House. He and his wife Suzanne have commiserated with me about everything, sick child, stolen car, vanished sabbatical. Now he is coming to look at the house. The Whites are thinking about moving from their present apartment, and I've offered to suggest them as tenants to the Walters. Some guilt sits on my shoulders. We rented from our friends, who were expecting a year's rent; here we are reneging. It would feel easier to find them a set of reliable tenants and pull them out of the

207

lurch. As we walk, a police car stops at the curb. The constable calls, "We found your car."

I look at Paul. "That's mighty excellent service. Can you see that happening in Massachusetts? Three hours I've known it was gone."

"It's in the middle of a farmer's field."

Goddamn kids. "Is it damaged?"

"It's difficult to say. We'll get him to pull it out with his tractor and see if we can get it over here for you."

"Thank you very much."

Paul leaves before the Maxi is brought back. He is doubtful about renting the house, but says they'll talk it over. After he goes, I call British Air and get a seat for Wednesday at 3:00 P.M. Then I do some laundry and fold sheets. About noon the constable brings the Maxi home.

It looks like an old pensioner after a hard carouse: body mud-spattered and scratched, right fender crumpled against the tire, headlight smashed. Inside a few items are gone—a plastic steering wheel cover, a petrol can—but there wasn't much to take in the first place. The radio is intact, but it has never worked anyway. The engine—faithful heartbeat!—still runs fine, and with a couple of swipes of a hammer to the fender, driving is possible. What has been destroyed, of course, is any resale value. "New wing, new headlamp," Mr. Young will call out as he inspects the damaged items; and their cost and that of the two-week-old clutch will easily exceed anything I can expect to get for the car.

By the time Monday comes, my ducks are in a row. I have packed and mailed a couple boxes of books. The computer is apart, separated from its British power adaptor and packed into boxes and cases. The top floor and the boys' bedrooms are clean down to the paint. All the sheets save mine are washed and folded. The garden is tidy.

As I have worked, anger has been curiously absent. My emotions have been hard to pin down: not despair nor even frustration, yet certainly not pleasure. I am not happy, not unhappy either. Suddenly it comes to me that at last for the first time in longer than I can remember I'm not trying to avoid thinking about Gardner. I am not only coping with adversity, but even prevailing over it. For six weeks I have been boxing with bees. In the last five days I have finished my work on Hardy, lost and recovered a car, and halfway cleaned the house. We made the right decision; even the doctor backed us up. The hell with the car.

Furthermore, the others are coping, too. Jane called again on Sunday night. "He's clearly better. He's eating boxes of cereal and holding them down. He's even swimming a little in Sarah's pool." I remember the friends they are staying with have a small indoor pool.

She had talked with the school about our house. "We'll be able to move back in a week or so after you get back. I haven't met the Spanish couple, but they seem to have been very nice about it all."

When I told her about the car, she laughed—a bit sardonic, but a laugh nonetheless. "Whew. You really are trying for the Job award, aren't you?"

"It's drivable," I said. "But not for a long trip or at night. I'm going to take it down to Mr. Young tomorrow for an evaluation. He knows what a good clutch it has."

"Right," she snorted. "Oh, well. Do the best you can." She pauses. "Ah, the Sabbatical From Hell. See you on Wednesday. We love you."

Yesterday I also got a call from Agnes, who wants to go to the Hardy play tonight. Normally I don't see her on Mondays, so I gave her directions to Hereford House, she agreed to drive, and I said I'd take her to dinner. Tomorrow night I'm to eat at the Browns and go to a lecture in Kidlington given by Colin Dexter, the author of the Inspector Morse mysteries. On Wednesday morning, Paul White will drive me to the airport.

This morning while cleaning, I picked up the £10 book coupon Jane received for speaking at the Oxford Women's Theology Seminar. She did not use it when she bought the new *Revised Standard Version Bible*, after all. After my Dickens lecture I stop at Blackwells to cash it in for a hardback copy of *The Wench is Dead*, Colin Dexter's latest Inspector Morse mystery. The dust jacket indicates that it is a sort of *Daughter of Time*, in which Morse solves a murder over one hundred years old while in the John Radcliffe Hospital. As a former historian, Jane will appreciate it, as a Morse fan she will enjoy it, and as a recent Oxford-area resident and John Radcliffe customer she will see it all too sharply in her mind's eye.

Agnes picks me up around five-thirty, and we head north to Coventry, about an hour and a half away. Like most drivers in England, she moves along at a brisk clip until after a time we find ourselves behind a rare slowpoke. She says, "Tell me if I should overtake this car, all right?"

"What?" Only then do I realize what has been nagging at me since we started. The oncoming cars are coming straight at me and I am sitting where the driver should be.

She laughs. "I brought my car from Germany."

"How do you keep yourself on the left? I have to start off every morning saying, 'Drive on the left,' and I have the right-hand drive to remind me."

"Oh, you get used to it."

As we pass through the dusk, I tell her the good news about my son, that he is eating, and the less good but certain news about the family, that we will not be returning to England. Then we chat about Austen and Hardy, Emma and Tess, Oxford and Germany and the United States. The mood is not doleful, not at all, as we roll toward Coventry.

We arrive in plenty of time and find a car park. A map guides us from an older section of the city—one that Lady Godiva might have gazed nakedly upon—across thoroughfares to more modern plazas, past neon windows of compact discs and jeans and articles of leather. The Belgrade Theater is large and new, though not lovely: glass and chrome and tile and all-weather carpeting, an extension of the shopping malls through which we have been walking. It contains a bar and a restaurant. After buying tickets, we drink a beer at the former and I make reservations for after the performance at the latter. Finally we take our seats.

For the next two hours, Tess Durbeyfield and Angel Clare and Alec D'Urberville and all the rest play out their tragedies. The adaptation tells virtually the entire story through a series of vignettes. Its impulse to omit as little as possible from the novel—in the abstract a virtuous one—becomes something of a liability, as the story disjoints. The vignettes rocket by, forcing the actors to play broad. When Tess's father announces to the family that they are not nobodys but descended from the old and noble D'Urbervilles, she mugs and grins along with the rest; in the book, I recall, she was scornful of the idea from the start.

Still, it's fun to watch. It's a powerful story, the actors are enjoying themselves, and when the shadows of the huge Stonehenge trilithons, so recently visited, loom on the screen above the exhausted couple, the great forces Hardy unleashed upon his characters turn visible and awful before us.

The next day I attend my final lecture from Professor Bayley. He has come to *Far From the Madding Crowd*, *The Hand of Ethelberta*, and *The Return of the Native* in his chronology. The thesis he presents concerning the first of these is that Hardy has created, out of elements of both comedy and tragedy, a "heroic pastoral." The sword exercise where Sergeant Troy dazzles Bathsheeba, brilliantly slicing the air around her but never touching her, comes close to comedy with "heroic exaggeration." The use of coincidence—Fanny's missing her wedding to Troy by going to the wrong church, for example, or his work on her grave destroyed by a storm the very night he completes it—creates an effect he describes as the "heroic grotesque." My notes are filled with the word "heroic."

"Having dis-dis-discovered this marvelous heroic pastoral in *Fa-Fa-Far From the Madding Crowd*, Hardy promptly gave it up with *The Hand of Ethelberta*." Although he passes over this book quickly—"Ha-Hardy was out of his element"—I am struck by one remark: Ethelberta, the butler's daughter who has moved upstairs with her rich mother-in-law is a "tra-transsexual version of Thomas Hardy himself, the young man on the ma-make, on the way up."

As the hour is nearly up when he comes to *The Return of the Native*, he promises to return to it next week. But he does give some grist for me, who will be an ocean away by then. One of my grand passions in fiction, Eustacia Vye, is Hardy's "most successful Madame Bovary," a characterization that pleases me. He goes on to assert that the book addresses the notion of travel—as of Diggory Venn the reddleman and Clym Yeobright the native. It is wearying, travel is, wearing away human hopes and desires. Time is a sort of travel, also, as the days and seasons wheel into darkness and winter. Then before I can anchor myself to my notebook, I am lost in his words and Hardy's ideas, traveling and wearing away too, dreaming of my traveled and weary little boy back home.

At nine o'clock in the evening I am in Kidlington listening to Colin Dexter, a witty, accomplished man, small, white-haired, linked to the world by a hearing aid in each ear. I ate dinner with the Browns, having arrived at their house with a great box of food, mostly from my wife's last big trip to Tesco. Also in the box, bound for their freezer, were eight quarts of blackberries I had picked from the embankment. "When we come back to visit," I told them, "we want native bramble tart." The Browns didn't want to hear Mr. Dexter but offered to drop me at the lecture hall and pick me up afterward.

The methodology of writing mysteries is explained, with allusions to Conan Doyle, Wilkie Collins, and others—nothing new, really, but several amusing anecdotes. During the question period at the end, I ask if John Thaw, the actor who plays Morse on television, has changed the author's conception of the character.

"No," he says. "Not at all. We agree about Morse. But Kevin Whately, who plays Lewis, has altered his character a great deal. In my first books Lewis was old, Morse's age. But the producers wanted more of a contrast between the two for television, so they brought in a younger man, from the north. Now I don't have Lewis making so many references to his grandchildren any more."

213

Afterward I bring up the copy of *The Wench is Dead* and tell him who it is for. He is very kind. He writes: "For Jane—with my best wishes to you—Colin Dexter 30.10.90."

The next morning Paul White drives me to the airport. I give him a final present: the bicycle. It's not beautiful, but it works. We talk about our futures, about what the remainder of the year holds for each of us as our paths careen apart. His car is stuffed with my five huge pieces of luggage: two duffel bags, three large cases, backpack, and briefcase. On my hand in ink I have listed them all. God knows how many times I have said to myself, "Do not lose the fucking briefcase."

Behind me Hereford House is as clean as I can make it, everything made ready for the new tenants, whoever they may be— not, however, the Whites, who have decided to stay where they are. I have spent these few days saying good-bye to people we have met here during our two and a half months: friends, fellow students, tradespeople, librarians, naturalist acquaintances. I called Dr. Gillian Forrest, to explain why we missed our appointment. I went to the Woodstock Primary School and talked long with Mrs. Tattam, thanking her for her support. I requested a telephone reading and an electric bill. I paid for a forwarding request at the post office. I said good-bye to the Browns, Martyn and Jane, Harriet and Peter, whom my family will never forget, nor cease to love.

Finally I sold the car for £100 to Mr. Young, who had found someone who would buy it for the MOT and the license disk, which still has eleven months of its £100 to run.

I am surprised at how pleased I am to be free of the Maxi. There is no bitterness there, I am sure; I don't even begrudge the pimply little bastard that stole it. This is not a time to worry about pounds and pence. I am cutting free, and I am leaving behind pain, I know it.

At Heathrow Paul helps me unload. I thank him profusely, wish him luck, and wave good-bye. In the terminal I pay for my ticket, check the luggage, and pass through security. Once in the waiting area I take out of the briefcase *Jude the Obscure,* which I have recently dared to begin. It is the last of Hardy's novels left for me, and I actually feel ready for it. It is partly set at the northern edge of Wessex, in Christminster, which is Hardy's name for Oxford. Jude Frawley is a stonecutter who dreams of greater things, of going to the university to become a scholar. His story is dark with terror—with fractured dreams, with failure, and incidentally with three dead children. I know this, having read it before. As a boy standing on a ladder one evening, Jude looks toward the city of his restless desires:

"Some way within the limits of the stretch of landscape, points of light like the topaz gleamed. The air increased in transparency with the laps of minutes, till the topaz points showed themselves to be the vanes, windows, roof slates, and other shining spots upon the spires, domes, freestonework, and varied outlines that were faintly revealed. It was Christminster, unquestionably; either directly seen or miraged in the peculiar atmosphere."

Then Jude's vision dims in a presentiment of the darkness that will ultimately consume his tragic future:

"The spectator gazed on and on till the windows and vanes lost their shine, going out almost suddenly like extinguished candles. The vague city became veiled in mist. Turning to the west, he saw that the sun had disappeared. The foreground of the scene had grown funereally dark, and near objects put on the hues and shapes of chimaeras."

A week ago these words would have brought me to my knees. But my life is not Jude's, my fading Oxford not his fading Christminster. Across the Atlantic it is Halloween, a different sort of evening of chimaeras; yet against the advent of that darkness I fly westward hopefully, toward the sun, toward home.

Epilogue

We adults, especially those of us
who are not smack in the middle of child raising, tend to think of
children as plastic, pliant creatures, ones we can mold into perfect images that reflect our perfect selves. The younger the child,
the easier the task, we say; just bend the twig and the bough
will grow true. Consider how we judge a child's behavior. When
my sons misbehave in public, throw tantrums in the middle of
a church service, say, I am mortified because I know everyone
else is saying, "He doesn't know the first thing about raising
children." When they mind their manners, say please and thank
you, I trust everyone else is thinking, "Ah, what well-brought-up
young gentlemen." My success as a parent—both in the minds of
others and in my own mind—so often is measured by the amount
of control I have over my children, how easily or not I can bend
them to my wise will.

This sounds Victorian, but I'm afraid it isn't. Before my wife
and I were parents, we were visiting the Washington Zoo on
a warm Saturday. We overheard a father, flush-faced and grim,
leaning over three sour children under the age of eight, state em-

217

phatically, "All right, damn it. We *will* have a good time today."

How we chortled! We would never speak to our children in such a fashion. They would be raised on love and logic, drawn ineluctably toward the right and the true and the good, toward, in short, whatever we wanted of them. My God, what naive and simple creatures we were! We should have been placed in an exhibit next to the snipes and the rails.

For the truth is something else. A parent's control over a child is limited, in some areas sharply so, unless the child voluntarily defers to authority. It is emblematic of how we value a pliant nature in a child that we call such children "easy." Yet in the abstract we forget how rare these natures are. Most of us embrace the romantic notion that childhood is a time of innocence and pleasure:

> And all the earth is gay;
> Land and sea
> Give themselves up to jollity,
> And with the heart of May
> Doth every Beast keep holiday:—
> Thou Child of Joy,
> Shout round me, let me hear thy shouts, thou happy
> Shepherd-boy!
> —William Wordsworth,
> "Ode: Intimations of Immortality"

When we were planning our trip to England, I never once thought we would encounter serious trouble from Gardner. For all his history of tantrums, of stubbornness, of inflexibility, I saw no hint of the difficulties that lay before us. He would find new friends in school. He would be stimulated by the excitement of the new country. Above all, he would receive support and love from his wonderful parents.

The word "luck" haunts me. It seems that we had none in England. If so, when we returned to the United States, it was there waiting for us. Friends took us in; the school moved us back into our house and gave us some assistance to recover from the numbing financial bath we had taken. I was able to keep my sabbatical going, reading Wordsworth, the Brontës, Anthony Powell; doing some additional travel; writing a manuscript about a child who went to England and there stopped eating. Jane continued to read, meditate, and pray. Over the year she led a workshop on Christian education and attended a couple of retreats at a nearby Episcopal monastery, of which she has since become an associate. Sam's vocabulary quickly outstripped "goggie" and "eep." Language exploded from him. As he turned two, he began speaking in paragraphs, not merely sentences, and for the most part with clarity, though for a long time the letter "L" eluded him—he lusted (still does) for "wolliepops"—and he was sometimes prone to spoonerism—one book of farm vehicles contained a picture of a "wivetock struck."

And what of Gardner, the man-at-arms, alone and palely loitering? In a word or four he is well again. He began eating immediately, even before we regained our house, chowing down cereals mostly, gaining a quarter-pound the first week back, and retrieving all his lost weight within two months. He entered kindergarten successfully, where he reestablished relationships with old friends and began some new ones. During that first summer back he went to several short stints of day camps: soccer camp, baseball camp, tennis camp, and camp camp, where at the campfire he won the Golden Marshmallow Award.

The story of Gardner's return and recovery, then, will be a happy one—and I am reminded that "happy" comes from "hap," which means chance or luck. That does not mean a god came down from the machine, tapped Gardner on the shoulder, and said, "Bibbity, bobbity, boo; go to the ball." The fact is we have spent a great deal of time and energy trying to unravel the emotional tangle left by the events of the fall of 1990. We began by attacking the emotional disarray enveloping all four of us.

Mental health services in this country are very rich, at times bewilderingly so. Generally speaking, there are three orders of counselors—choirs, thrones, dominions: licensed clinical social workers (who often write L.C.S.W. or L.I.C.S.W. after their names), clinical psychologists (with M.A. or Psy.D. or Ph.D. after theirs), and psychiatrists (M.D.). We met with all three at different stages of our journey. As mentioned in the narrative, even before my return from England Jane had found a clinical social worker with a practice in family counseling.

The ecology of our family—that fine balance of give and take between the various members—lay in tatters. Neither Jane nor I had been able to say "no" to our older son for two months, so desperate had we been to find some way to make him eat, make him sleep, make him happy. As in any household with one child ill for a significant period, the rest of the family had been hobbled by the necessity of deferring to the invalid. Often the counselor used the word "control" to describe what our son had been doing, a word that I first did not understand, for to me the idea of control has always had the element of conscious or deliberate manipulation. "To lose control" of a situation is to lose the ability to guide it, and a guide by definition knows where to go. Gardner was out of control, yet for two months he had been pushing buttons and turning wheels, a blind pilot gone amok, controlling uncontrollably, helplessly steering the ship straight onto the shoals.

The licensed clinical social worker got us back in balance. He did so very quickly, after three or four meetings with us and six or seven with Gardner. We turned to him for advice; when we wondered if a family trip to Vermont would be a good idea, he said, "Do you want to go? Then go." (It may be a measure of how bewildered we were that we felt the need to ask this question.) Before Christmas—that is, in two months—he told us that in his view we no longer needed him.

Of course we asked him for an explanation of what had happened and a prognosis. He seemed to think the event had been characterological. "With him you will never have a flexible son," he said. But he did not think that Gardner needed further therapy. "He's bright and verbal. He has all the tools to cope." Already we were seeing improvement. He was gaining weight. Around Thanksgiving he had begun to attend kindergarten and for three days a week an after-school program, both with obvious enthusiasm.

The kindergarten could not have been more different from the one in England. Our town offered an Early Learning Center in one of its elementary schools, gathering together all the kindergartners in town, along with the Readiness Group (those children who need an extra year before first grade) and a testing and intervention center. When Gardner arrived, he was tested and we were interviewed; afterward, he was placed in a classroom that contained a wise, experienced teacher and a number of his friends from last year. His progress was carefully monitored in light of his recent experiences. We have never felt so fortunate.[*]

Throughout the winter he did well, bringing home a report

[*]Sadly in these days of budget cutting, our town has dismantled the Early Learning Center, as an expensive educational bauble. We were greatly distressed. What a wonderful tool it was, not just for our son's salvation but for the innumerable problems of other children which it was able to isolate and intervene with. We would maintain that such a program would pay for itself many times over by the time a generation of students has passed beyond its doors.

that put him safely at grade level. His temper, a cause of concern in earlier years, seemed under better control than ever. I was ready to forgive and forget the whole thing, figuring why try to fix what seemed to have fixed itself. Jane, however, would not play ostrich; she wanted to know as much as possible about what had caused our dreadful English autumn and to act, if necessary, so that it might not recur. In March she got him an appointment with a child psychiatrist for a full evaluation. About this time an event occurred that suggested she was right, that his recovery had not reached the roots of whatever had been wrong.

He was invited to participate in his aunt's wedding. This was the aunt who had written to him in England, and he has always been very fond of her. In order to be in the wedding he would have to wear a sports coat, gray slacks, and a tie—clothing which he had never, voluntarily or otherwise, been asked to wear in his life. He wanted to be in the wedding, but he wanted nothing to do with the clothes, and he went back and forth in agonies of indecision.

Finally he said yes—much to my surprise—and he and Jane went to Brooks Brothers to be fitted for the clothes.

He couldn't do it. Jane reported that in the store he absolutely came apart, falling to the floor, weeping and flailing. Somehow he was riven between intention and execution, between desire and consummation. His failure yawned in front of me, and I thought of the opening of Eliot's *Ash-Wednesday:*

> Because I do not hope to turn again
> Because I do not hope
> Because I do not hope to turn
> Desiring this man's gift and that man's scope
> I no longer strive to strive towards such things

"Let's see what the psychiatrist says," I said.

A psychiatrist is, of course, a physician, who may employ both medical and psychotherapeutic techniques to diagnose and treat patients. The one we saw met with us for three sessions together, one with each parent separately, and five with Gardner. Jane and I talked about our family histories and our lives with our children. Gardner played and drew.

The doctor also arranged for him to be tested by a clinical psychologist. Such testing is the easiest to report on, for it involves quantification; and Gardner's quantities were revelatory. The testing was divided into two areas, cognitive (intelligence) and projective (personality). In the former, Gardner showed himself—as his parents so hopefully expected—to be a bright six-year-old boy: "initially quite verbal, engaging, communicative, and expressive." Even so, there were two weaknesses that appeared on the Wechsler Intelligence Scale for Children (WISC)—a test which, because of its subtests, allows some discrimination in evaluating areas of cognitive development. The "digit span" and the "coding" subtests were significantly lower than the others, suggesting as the report noted "relatively poor auditory short-term memory and attention skills. Also, a significantly lower score on the Coding subtest may be due to weaker speed of eye-hand coordination, weaker visual short-term memory, or lowered motivation to perform on this rote learning task." Although we wanted to leap upon this last option—he was bored, too bright for rote learning—we knew that he had not been bored in England.

In the personality testing, the psychologist discovered a radically different child from the bright articulate one above: "Gardner's responses to projective testing suggest that the level of his emotional coping and resources is well below his advanced cognitive abilities. . . . He is a child who is easily made anxious and

223

for whom emotions can easily get stirred up and overwhelming. Once emotionally aroused, he shows limited resources to cope and contain his affect. His basic coping stance is to attempt to 'block out' the unwanted feeling and to wait for it to dissipate and go away."

Reading these words was at first difficult, but today I am only astonished at how apposite they are. The psychologist went on: "Gardner is a sensitive child who is highly reactive to emotions which he tends to experience strongly and intensely. . . . Anger is the predominant affect of concern based on test responses. Anger and aggression are quite frightening to him, and he cannot tolerate viewing himself as an angry or aggressive person."

We met separately with both doctors to hear their reports, for we did not want either to screen the other. Not surprisingly, they both agreed on most of what they saw. "He contains anger he doesn't know how to deal with," said the psychiatrist. Both said he felt guilty for bringing us home. They did not exactly concur on the nature of treatment they would prescribe, but in making their recommendations, both described perfectly the little boy we knew. Finally both were optimistic. "He's very verbal and very cooperative," said the psychiatrist. "He should benefit greatly." They both made sense. We had been saying since we got home that it was better to deal with this sort of thing at six than at sixteen. "We'd better start dealing with it, then," said Jane. "Don't you agree?"

Each session had cost around $100 apiece. Our health-care plan paid for the first $500 a year for mental health costs. The psychiatrist had recommended that we establish Gardner in a course of therapy that would require one or two meetings a week for probably two years at minimum. Facing a medical bill that would total somewhere between five and ten thousand big ones a year, we hastily changed to a health plan with a larger allocation for mental health treatment and at the same time placed one-third of my salary into a flexible spending account, which meant we could have our unreimbursed medical expenses paid back with pretax dollars. Then we went looking for a therapist.

I now think that choosing a psychological counselor/therapist is a crapshoot, but we began like scholars. First, we read to learn the differences among the various types of counselors, the L.I.C.S.W.'s with their tools of contract and arbitration, the psychologists with theirs of stimulation and behavior modification, and the psychiatrists with play therapy and pharmacopoeia. We spoke with friends and colleagues, for the school where I teach has an impressive staff of psychological counselors. We looked through the list of psychological therapists on our new health-care plan's roster and interviewed some of them. Still, when at last we chose, it was luck that brought us to the doctor we found, a kind, communicative, intelligent man with a wide range of clinical experience. He proved to be a generalist, incorporating techniques from all the psychotherapeutic disciplines—"If it makes sense, I use it," he said—working with Gardner, with us, and with his first-grade teacher to attack the various issues the testing had uncovered. It was he who urged me to speak clearly with Gardner about the spanking in the bathroom, thus allowing each of us to begin to purge our shame and guilt.

The Woodstock Primary School had been so clearly the catalyst in initiating his anorexia that we expected the worst when we entered him in the school system back here. All things considered, he has done very well. He has maintained grade level and improved in some of his weaknesses. He has had two excellent teachers who have attended him with patience and insight, and this year is enthusiastic about his new one. The WISC scores, however, suggested two areas that initially gave him trouble and that have continued to do so. First, reading has not come easily.

The low score of the coding subtest has been reflected in his difficulty in recognizing and remembering words. His school gave him some retesting this past year, the results of which were consistent with the earlier data. He has been receiving tutoring in reading, with success; the school psychologist writes, "His Title I tutor and teacher both report progress despite his difficulties."

Second, a larger cognitive issue has to do with his attention span. I had never heard of Attention Deficit Disorder (ADD) before his psychiatrist gave us a pamphlet describing it: "a condition wherein children, adolescents, or adults show inappropriate degrees of attention, impulsiveness, and sometimes hyperactivity." Gardner displays many of the symptoms listed in the pamphlet, such as fidgeting, talking out of turn, interrupting, failing to listen. One passage in the pamphlet leaped out at us: "You may be wondering how [such distractible behavior] fits with the times when you observe your child attending to something for extended periods of time. Often these are situations where he or she is doing something that is enjoyable like building with Legos." We were spun back to Bristol, to the Lego exhibit, to the sad shrunken boy who sat snapping those little colored bricks together; and we could not doubt that this shoe fit.

His therapist has been quick to point out that Gardner's ADD is borderline. Tests given by both our psychologist and the school's have placed him at the extreme of the normal range, which means that he is affected by the condition but not driven by it. We have been considering medication, but he has been doing well without it, and we would prefer that he develop his own coping mechanisms if he can. For the present we will keep monitoring his progress and his happiness.

So now he is growing stronger. He gets along well with his little brother, certainly as well as most other pairs of three- and seven-year-olds. They shared a bedroom this summer and enjoyed each other greatly. He has entered second grade and the seven-and eight-year-olds' soccer league enthusiastically. Two of his old friends came over after the first game and racketed around for several hours, young chimps in The Peaceable Kingdom. He gets angry sometimes and stomps around and yells. But he recovers quickly. He acts just like a seven-year-old boy. I know what is inside him, and I still feel he acts just like a seven-year-old boy.

I have provided this profile of my son for several reasons. First, it shows how much I have learned about him—and by extrapolation how little I knew before we went to England. Before that, he was plastic on the way to the mold, a gob of soft wax waiting to be imprinted by the Great Seal of Life. He was bright, he was handsome, and even though he was at times difficult, he was my son, whom I would raise to be an image of my own wise and handsome self. And this is why I am describing him to you, because I do not think my perceptions are very much different from yours, nor that he is very much different from your child. Since I have been home, I have met other people whose young children, faced with overwhelming loss—of a home, of a friend, of a parent or sibling—have stopped eating. Five-year-old children *do* have eating disorders, despite what the English doctor said. And if they do become images of our wise and handsome selves, it is not our will that effects the transition. It is theirs.

To some extent, understanding the story of my son's anorexia is complicated by a problem inherent in listening to narrative. Every story speaks with an idiosyncratic yet polyglot voice. I am not here referring to the narrator, whose voice recounts the events. I mean the sound all the characters and events make as they play upon and against each other like the musicians and instruments of a symphony orchestra. This sound does not arrive in a sentence such as "I want to go home," not even when the sentence is qualified by clauses beginning with "because." Partly this happens because many characters—parents, children, friends, doctors—speak during the course of a narrative. None of them, including even the narrator, can be presumed to understand the complete logic of the story being told.

While I have been writing this story, I have all the time been consulting with my wife. Her journal has guided me through the sequence of events, some of which I might have forgotten, others I might have preferred to. More importantly, her insights have often led me to emphasize certain incidents I might otherwise have discounted or omitted altogether. Still, reading through the pages I have written, she has remarked often that my story is not hers. I have not always been true to her. Her role as planner, for instance, feels faint in my narrative; yet she worked out almost every family event we were able to accomplish in England. We would not have gone to any fairs or castles or exhibitions without her, and she had arranged some others—a week in Wales in December, for example—that we were forced to abandon. A more significant aspect of her story that I have not been able to recount with any substance is simply the happiness she experienced while we were there. Her story is not all, or even largely, pain. I know her joys existed for I saw them; yet in my narrative I have shown my joys in detail, merely indicating vaguely, all too much I fear, that both professionally and personally the power of the spirit gave her much in which to rejoice.

To what degree have I misrepresented my son? I have no idea. He has not been read a word of this book, so has had no opportunity even to disagree with it. We have perceived him as unhappy, even despairing, for much of his time in England. Probably this is true. But how conscious was he of what he felt? All we have is the narrative, my narrative, this narrative. It must suffice.

The fact is, stories—whether fictional or factual—speak to us largely by the conjoining of phenomena. These may be words spoken, but they are also deeds done and much else besides. "Each event spoke with a cryptic tongue," notes Richard Wright in his autobiographical *Black Boy*. This is another way of saying that in narrative we are informed by symbol, the discovery of meaning in events and objects. My five-year-old son watched a film of an extraterrestrial far from its home growing pale and wizened, and cryptic tongues wagged furiously at the rest of us. Too furiously? Perhaps. Although the tongues themselves may have been cryptic—who or what shapes their speech?—their messages seem to have been remarkably consistent: "Take the poor little blighter home," they said over and over. But in the last analysis, I don't believe that what we were given was solely, or even primarily, an injunction to act.

During the spring while I was writing the first draft of this book, I gave a reading of some of its sections to a group of students at my school. They were wonderfully attentive listeners, not only sympathetic but clearly empathetic as well. (At least two members of the audience, I knew, had battled anorexia themselves.) Afterward one girl asked, "What do you think the effect of your book will be on Gardner? Do you worry about exposing him in it?"

"Yes. Yes, I do," I said at once. Other fathers have earned the frank and open anger of their children for writing about them. Christopher Milne could never forgive his father, and who can blame him?

Hush, hush, whisper who dares,
Christopher Robin is saying his prayers.

Who could forgive one's father for writing those lines? Not I. Imagine the teasing in the schoolyard. Every year one would have to fight every loudmouth in every grade all over again.

To the questioner I mentioned two books I had recently read. The first was William Styron's *Darkness Visible*, in which a nearly fatal attack of clinical depression is rendered so tangible as to be comprehensible even to someone who has never tasted its bitter mist. He describes his recovery, turning at last to Dante emerging from the Inferno: "For those who have dwelt in depression's dark wood, and known its inexplicable agony, their return from the abyss is not unlike the ascent of the poet, trudging upward and upward out of hell's black depths and into what he saw as 'the shining world.'"

Certainly other people have been helped by reading such a sensitive and powerful narrative as Styron's. Hope is hard to keep away when the despairing read that others like themselves have been healed. My son's story is not unique, and his way of showing loss, of grieving, may be an extreme example of a common enough pattern of behavior. Indeed, my questioner herself, after the reading was over, told me that she had behaved similarly during a year in Italy. And a woman in the school's business office mentioned to me that her first-grade son had stopped eating for a time after they moved to a town ten miles north. The pain of this story is, I am sure, to be found in many others; and to share pain—one's own or someone else's—is in some measure to alleviate it.

The second book I referred to was *Telling Secrets* by Frederick Beuchner. When Beuchner was ten, his father committed suicide; less than a month later his mother moved him and his brother to Bermuda, never to mention the event again. They kept it secret, where it secretly festered and kept them secretly unwell. Forty years later he wrote obliquely of this sad death, and

230

after a while he realized that his writing had begun to heal him: "through the power that memory gives us of thinking, feeling, imagining our way back through time we can at long last finally finish with the past in the sense of removing its power to hurt us and other people and to stunt our growth as human beings."

Here is the most basic reason to write this narrative, for all its flaws and partial truths: it has the power to heal. It can reveal to me and my family truths about what did and did not happen, and it can allow us to tell further truths to each other. Let me give an example of each possibility.

Constantly during our time in England, when things were getting rougher and rougher, we asked ourselves *why?* What was the cause, we wondered, and as things got even worse, we wanted to know who or what we could blame. *Blame:* searching out the great scapegoat, we turned upon England, upon the absence of a car, the presence of the vertically mixed first class at the primary school, the lethargy of Federal Express or the National Health System, the lack of Corn Pops or salted popcorn. Failing the extrinsic, we turned upon ourselves: not enough love, not enough flexibility, not enough money, not enough discipline. Or, worst of all, we turned wordlessly upon the child: inflexible, angry, selfish. But blame is a canard, after all, a wild goose.

A pattern may be described in the events of this narration; a causal relationship between them may be discerned. Even fault may be affixed to them, but not blame. Blame, unlike fault, requires intent. I can blame you for hurting me only if you did so purposefully, or at least negligently. And in this story no one acts deliberately or carelessly in order to hurt another. There is no villain. Not even I who have said and done such terrible things to my five-year-old son.

Seeing this, we realize that—though we may be at fault—we are without blame, all of us who participated in this narrative.

231

And with this realization guilt breaks away from our souls like clay in a torrent of water, and we are free to grow whole again and love each other once more.

And here, at last, is what I can tell my son, who has caused me to hear the voice of this narrative, to attend to it and write it down so all can hear it too. I observed earlier that this voice was not simply telling us to act, that is, to take him home. Instead we were being asked finally to believe and accept, or more precisely, to trust and let go. In the film *Longtime Companion,* the character played by Bruce Davison, coaching his lover who is dying of AIDS, says with exquisite gentleness and compassion and love: "Let go, now. Ah, dear. Just let it go." Letting go of anything— of life, certainly, but also of dreams and fictions, of friends and lovers, of places, even of a small object like a Teenage Mutant Hero Turtle—demands faith, often great faith. We must put fear aside. As I have said, we must listen. And we must, my son, love: you, your mother, your brother, even I, all of us, yes.